Uncle Martin's Sister

Uncle Martin's Sister

A Memoir of Friendships Past

Route 3, Stockbridge, Georgia — and Other Places, 1906–1917

Dorothea Whitaker McAlvin

MOUNTAIN ARBOR
       PRESS
Alpharetta, GA

The author has tried to recreate events, locations, and conversations from her memories of them. In some instances, in order to maintain their anonymity, the author has changed the names of individuals and places. She may also have changed some identifying characteristics and details such as physical attributes, occupations, and places of residence.

Copyright © 2022 by Dorothea McAlvin

All rights reserved. No part of this book may be reproduced or transmitted in any form or by any means, electronic or mechanical, including photocopying, recording, or any information storage and retrieval system, without permission in writing from the author.

ISBN: 978-1-6653-0231-9

Library of Congress Control Number: 2021924434

Printed in the United States of America   1 2 3 0 2 1

∞This paper meets the requirements of ANSI/NISO Z39.48-1992 (Permanence of Paper)

To the Memory of Aunt Betty,
Martin's real sister

Elizabeth Ardella Wilson, 1882–1968

The dutiful daughter
The unmarried sister
The maiden aunt
The unassuming presence

The quiet laborer
In home and field
And in the Lord's vineyard

The keeper
The giver

The Name Unknown, The Life Unheralded

*He represents a family and a place—the family and the place
unknown and unheralded as much as he.*

But, surely, he is more than representative,

As are they all, the others of the family of no particular repute,

*And the others of the place never remarked upon in its time,
and now disappeared,
all character lost as days, months, years—
indeed, a century—have become another time.*

*Who was he?
You, though you lived your first decade during his last,
You cannot know.*

*For you took scarce note of him then
And now ought remains:*

*A tombstone,
the dates inclusive—month, day, year:
the first, of birth; the second, of death.*

*What lies between you recall,
as for your parents, too.
Or you imagine or invent.
You pretend to know.*

*What say the marks upon a paper—records kept by church, reports
required by state, letters breathing life and love, friendship and hope,*

Sometimes with undertone of despair?

*For he IS.
More than representative.
Even if you get it wrong.
The portrait is worth the penning.*

Martin.

Contents

Chapter One
    The Long Decade   1

Chapter Two
    "Lots of things were different from what you thought them to be." Anna J., Flippen, Georgia, 1906 and 1908   5

Chapter Three
    "I would be better satisfied to continue going with you as heretofore." Anna, Riverdale, Georgia, 1906   15

The Anna Letters   22

Chapter Four
    "I desire that my brother Martin Alonzo Wilson be paid the sum of five dollars . . . out of my estate." Martin's Family   23

Chapter Five
    "It was the prayers . . . at old Noah's Ark that reached God." Martin's Church and Community   33

Chapter Six
    "The slaughter of the innocent does drive away good citizens." Atlanta, 1906   39

Chapter Seven
    "In the name of Jesus, get saved . . ." Mack Carnes, Asbury College, Wilmore, Kentucky, 1908   49

Chapter Eight
    "It will be to me as if all the rays of sunshine shut out of my life." Mag, Homer, Demorest, and Fowlstown, 1917   61

Chapter Nine
    "I think you are the most thoughtful boy . . ." Sister, Maysville and Lula, 1915 and 1916   73

Acknowledgments   113
Bibliography   115

Chapter One
THE LONG DECADE

When we first made a quick read-through of the letters written to our great uncle, Martin Wilson, we thought of course that the "Sister" who signed them with affection was his sister, Betty. The affection was there, in the letters' content, too—so much so that it gave us pause. Should a sister write so endearingly to a brother? Well, we said, it was a different era; these missives are over one hundred years old; perhaps in the mores of the time, that tone was permissible. It was easy enough, however, after a more careful reading, to determine that it couldn't have been Aunt Betty who had written them—though on that first reading we had hoped it was Aunt Betty. How different from the quiet, self-effacing maiden lady of advanced years was the lively and engaging woman who wrote these letters in the bloom of youth.

It was not the never-married farm woman, homemaker to two brothers in succession, who was hidden in that hand. We could not reconstruct Aunt Betty's life from the letters. We could not give it an outer form that would make our great aunt different from the woman whose memory we too-dimly carried. We could not speculate on her life's inner dimensions, either, for we had no starting point. Uncle Martin's "Sister," however, might be discovered. And, if we found her, we might find him. The writer's Martin was "the most thoughtful boy," though he had long outgrown boyhood by the time she was writing. He died when we were children, and, because to children any old person seems a given in their mind's scape, we never imagined him ever to have been young. His correspondent mentions this Martin playing tennis, too, and that seemed more incongruous yet. During the era of his youth, surely, tennis playing implied a country club or a college campus or a life with some leisure in it. We assumed his to have been, even in the decades of his youth, in the earliest years of the twentieth century, a life of toil: planting under the hot Georgia sun so that his neck turned red; plowing, half-harnessed himself, along with the mule, to the plow; hauling cotton by wagonload to the gin in nearby Flippen.

We have twelve letters that survived time's carelessness—and no way to know why Martin saved them. Born in 1878, two years before our grandfather, he was almost thirty years old when the first of those he saved was written (this one not from Sister), and he was one year shy of forty when he received the last of them (this one also not from Sister). The years 1906 to 1917 mark a long decade in his life, and there are things we find intriguing about his life in those years. There was, for instance, a mysterious illness that almost cost him his life. During the period, he had a strong interest in religion, or so his correspondents assumed (or hoped or dreaded), with one friend, this one a young man, urging him to find salvation before death should find him. The young women who were his friends were, as his mother had been before her marriage, teaching school somewhere. They wrote, all of them, almost without exception, about their schools, and they wrote about church and campgrounds and singings, and some worried about whether they—and he—were living the Christian life.

His correspondents lived in, or visited and invited him to visit, the far-flung corners of the state. There were letters from towns near his home—from Flippen in Henry County and from Riverdale in Clayton. But there were letters also from southwest Georgia's pine barrens—from Fowlstown, only fifty miles north of Tallahassee, Florida, and from the state's northeastern mountains as well. It is Sister who describes her home in Maysville as "in the mountains," though her hometown is in reality more piedmont than mountain, with mountains hardly visible except on drives away from there, on northerly routes toward Demorest and

Piedmont College. In Demorest and at Piedmont College, I hoped to find a connection, however tangential, to the last of Uncle Martin's correspondents, and, perhaps, to him.

At some point during the time covered by the letters, Martin moved from one farm to another. In 1900, he was living on his family's farm in Henry County, a farm laborer in his mother's employ. Our family's oral history tells of his going to Texas to work on a railroad after that 1900 date; our grandfather went with him. Our grandfather and another of Martin's brothers had married by 1910; each had become father to a child, and each had acquired his own farm. Their mother died early that year; the oldest brother, not yet married, assumed "head of household" status, and he, the unmarried brothers, and their sister worked the land together. The letters Martin received through 1916 were sent to that farm's address, Stockbridge, Georgia. Sister exclaims to him in one of those letters how thrilled she was to learn that there was a letter with a Stockbridge postmark awaiting her return to her Maysville home after time away.

Whatever happened to Sister and to their relationship, it is another young woman—whom we can know only as Mag—who wrote the last letters. Mag posts them to Jonesboro, the county seat of Clayton County. Martin's move from one address to another was a move of only a mile or so; it put him in a different county, but in possession of his own farm; county jurisdiction hardly mattered. On that farm, in the imposing house atop a hill, Martin lived a bachelor life, with Aunt Betty as housekeeper and farm helper. When he died in 1952, the funeral director, a family connection, laid his body on a narrow bed in the house and the family sat watch until the hour of the funeral.

Chapter Two
"LOTS OF THINGS WERE DIFFERENT FROM WHAT YOU THOUGHT THEM TO BE." ANNA J., FLIPPEN, GEORGIA, 1906 AND 1908

There are problems with discovering who wrote the letters to Uncle Martin. Some of them were saved with their envelopes, but the style of the time apparently did not include adding a return address, so we have no surname for any of the young women. Two letters are missing their last page—or pages—so they lack even a signature. We tried to match handwriting but sometimes found ourselves in disagreement over the sender's identity. Often, the writer would place the date at the head of the letter—or, in one case, at its end. But a letter might have only a "Thursday evening" or a "Monday morning" in place of a date, and, unfortunately for the investigators, these are the very letters that do not include the envelope that would have let us know the month, day, and year.

The letters from two women who shared the same name—Anna—have features in common. The handwriting is so similar—the cursive M so prettily the same, for example—that there was a time when I thought the two to be one. Both young women were "taking" a school at the time of their writing to Martin; it is to be hoped that the penmanship they taught their students was more legible than that in their personal, often hurried, often agitated, correspondence. That the letters came from different places does not argue against their having been penned by the same woman, for the places are not that far apart. Especially if she were boarding during the school year with a family relation, his correspondent would not have moved very far from home. I am admitting, therefore, that I have no good reason for assuming two Annas, beyond my own conjecture.

The earliest letter comes from Flippen—from Anna J. This Anna does not append the *J* to letters she writes after that first, but I will continue to use it to distinguish between the two Annas. (She does form the A differently, hers the triangular shape rather than the rounded, with a nice little flourish on the bottom left to support the letter's tilt rightward.) Anna J.'s Flippen is in Martin's home county, only a short distance away from the family farm on which he was living in 1906. Flippen has a railroad running through, and at the beginning of the last century there was a depot with passenger service. Near the railroad track, an old building or two survive to this day to indicate that the town was, in its time, a small-scale commercial and agri-business center. Indeed, Gene Morris, official historian of Henry County, describes Flippen, like the county's other settlements at the turn into the twentieth century, as a "self-sustaining" community:

> *Flippen could boast of a blacksmith shop . . . a cider manufacturer . . . a cotton gin . . . four general merchandise stores . . . two fertilizer dealers . . . a saw miller . . . a school, a depot (Southern Railway), a church (Flippen Methodist) and a post office. . .*[1]

Off the road that passes over the grade-level railroad crossing sat some fine houses. They were the homes of the local enterprisers and perhaps of some farmers whose land holdings were so scattered that it made better sense for them to live in a settlement rather than on one of those properties. To access the road that passes through Flippen, Martin had to make only one turn, a short distance eastward from his home, where the road empties into the

---

[1] Gene Morris Jr. *True Southerners. A Pictorial History of Henry County, Georgia.* (McDonough, GA. The Henry County Record, 2000), 70.

one that passes through Flippen. If he rode on horseback or in a wagon for about five miles or so, he would arrive at the little village's center. (I surmise that the family did not own a buggy, though perhaps it did—for going into town or to church.) The railway track and the depot lay ahead of him as he rode into the village—just beyond the Methodist church sitting on its slight rise of a hill at roadside, which he would have passed on his left.

Today, Flippen is an unincorporated part of Henry County, and the residents claim a McDonough address. The bustle of today comes from traffic as those residents, rushing from jobs anywhere in the metropolitan Atlanta area, crowd the state routes and Interstate 75 to make their way home to one of the many subdivisions—upscale as well as modest—that have replaced orchards, woods, pastures, and fields. After all, as the sign in the Southern Railway Depot had indicated, Flippen was only twenty-four rail-miles from Atlanta.

The first of Anna J.'s letters begins a new year; it is dated January 1, 1906. There is no New Year's greeting, but there had evidently been a party or gathering to mark the season. Perhaps a circle of friends in the Flippen area had been partying throughout Christmas week. One local history picturing that era has a fulsome account of Christmas and end-of-year and New Year's celebrations in those early years of the twentieth century:

> Christmas was the big event of the year. One whole week's vacation for everybody! . . . The holiday really began on Christmas Eve . . . when the kiddies hung up their stockings for Santa to fill . . . [with] little toys carved from wood with Daddy's knife, a pair of tom-walkers, rag dolls, ginger bread men, popcorn balls, and syrup candy made by mother.[2]

Among the teenagers (Martin was beyond his teen years; perhaps Anna J. was yet that young), the young ladies took turns

---

[2] *History of the City of Riverdale* ([Jonesboro, GA] n.d.), 11.

entertaining the crowd at dinner parties. "Crowd" is the right word to use, for often there were more than thirty at one place.

The young men were responsible for straw rides, and for a place to congregate each night. The Square Dance (sic) was in vogue at the time. All the prearrangement necessary for the evening entertainment was permission from the parents to meet in their homes. The young men took the beds down from one or two rooms, depending on the number of people present, sprinkled meal on the floor, thus making a satisfactory dance hall. After the party was over, the floors were swept and everything put back in its proper place, so that the host and hostess were not inconvenienced.

The dance music (harmonica, guitar, fiddle, and clapping) was furnished by the young men.

It wouldn't seem like Christmas without Fantastic Riding—that is, a crowd of young men and boys [who] wore comic masks and clothing, [who] tried to disguise their voices, and rode horseback to the homes in the community. These fantastics were welcomed and treated to cakes or fruit, while the spectators tried to identify the riders. Occasionally the children were frightened, then the masks were removed. When seeing the fantastics were people they knew, the kiddies were ready to enjoy all the others as they came, regardless of their hideous appearance.

This week of merriment closed with a Watch Party in some of the homes . . . Much of the entertainment is centered around the church. Usually a Christmas pageant is presented by the young people. This is followed by a tree for the children. The middle aged couples carry baskets of fruit to the elderly people, and boxes of bountiful supplies of food and clothing to the needy. (These boxes also contained toys and

Christmas goodies for the kiddies.) The young people go carol singing, thus spreading joy all over the town. Parties of various kinds are attended every night during the week, but the Watch Party is held at the church, where singing, games and contests are enjoyed. Of course refreshments are served, then the New Year is ushered in with a very impressive devotional service, usually one of rededication.[3]

If there had been a week of partying—dinners in various houses and straw rides and square dancing and fantastic riding—during this particular Christmas season, Anna J. mentions nothing of it in her brief note. Nor does she allude to a church Watch Night service. But there had been a party, or perhaps a Watch Night service, and someone had said something untoward. Anna J. takes it upon herself to make amends—and while she is at it, she schedules a rendezvous:

Dear Mr. Martin,

You can't imagine my feelings this morning. You may not have taken acceptation (sic) to what was said last night. He said it not thinking that you would become offended and is very sorry.

You may rest assured that your visits here are appreciated and you have a hearty welcome by all. I hope you are not hurt with me in the least. I hope you will never mention it.

I am thinking of taking a school in a week or so, and I would like to have a talk with you next Sunday afternoon at two.

If you think there is anything amiss in me writing this note[, I] hope you will pardon the same.

Respectfully
Your Friend,
Anna J.

---

[3] *History of the City of Riverdale,* 12.

One letter from Anna J. has no clear date, but it seems to have come from Flippen. If she has taken a school, it must have been in the area. The letter is a quick reply to a letter Martin had written; it indicates some contretemps between them, and some mysterious "affair" that held interest for both of them. Indeed, the way she writes of the "affair" makes it almost appear that Martin is not so much a love interest as he is a gossipy confidant:

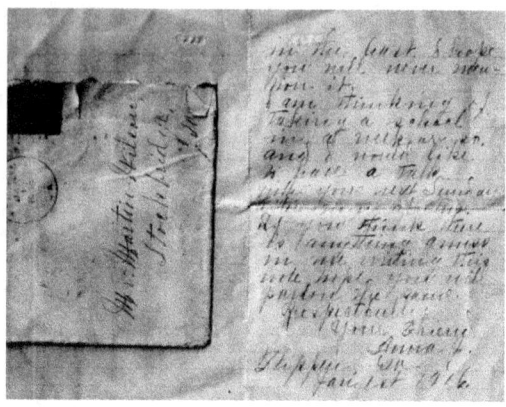

Excerpt from Anna J.'s Letter of January 1, 1906

> *Dear Martin,*
> *Yours of today received and will say in reply that the things you have heard are not true if they are harmful, and it will be impossible for me to see you at Robert's Monday night, but if you like you may come soon after dinner Saturday P.M. and go with Mattie Lucius and myself to put up our table at the Camp-ground. I am real anxious to hear what you have heard. Come prepared to relate the whole affair.*
>
> *Very hurriedly,*
Anna
Thursday 10 – 2 o'clock

In 1906, there was a Thursday, the tenth, in May; in 1907, there was one in January and another in October; in 1908, one in September. Anna J. was probably not corresponding with Martin as late as September 1908, however, as we shall see, so the occasion is probably set for the date in May in 1906, or, perhaps, in October 1907. The campground near Flippen was Shingleroof; it was usual for a camp meeting to be held in summer after the cotton was "laid by"; it was never held as late as October, for that was cotton picking time. Setting up a table, which Anna and her friend (or relation) are planning to do on a Saturday night, probably means a one-day event rather than a camp meeting, for folks set up tents, not tables, for camp meeting—and the setting up of tents meant that they moved into permanent structures surrounding the campground's tabernacle for a stay of a week or more. This letter clearly has something less than a camp meeting in mind.

If we assume a May 1906 date for the second letter, there is a two-year gap between it and the next from Anna J.—a gap that we can only fill with speculation. (If we propose an October 1907 date, there is still a gap, but a shorter one.) Speculation can only assume that in Anna J.'s mind, Martin had progressed, over the course of the months, from being a confidant to being someone for whom she cared. And now comes the realization that the caring might not be mutual. The letter is dated April 9, 1908—the date appearing at the end of the letter and on the envelope that had enclosed it. The envelope is postmarked Flippen, and it carries the notation, apparently added by the mail carrier, that it had been mis-sent to Route 2, Stockbridge, with Route 3 added for further direction. The writer had not included the route number (none of the envelopes seems to have had the route number).

In the letter there is mention of telephoning to another house to garner information—in this case about the progress of the illness from which Martin was suffering. When Sister is writing almost a decade later, she writes, rather as if it is no remarkable thing, about a telephone in her Maysville home. In rural areas like Anna J.'s, Sister's, and Martin's, even in the towns and not just in the more distant farming areas, I had assumed access to a telephone to have been rare. In Gene Morris's history of Henry County, however, the author describes the many telephone exchanges:

> Subscriber owned Telephone Companies were organized by farmers and merchants throughout Henry County . . . Henry County's pioneer telephone

entrepreneurs entered the business primarily so they could enjoy telephone service.

Farmers who lived along the telephone lines could qualify for telephone service by purchasing a share of stock [in the company]. Calls were charged for [on] a per call basis. These early Henry County telephone exchanges rarely had over a few dozen subscribers and line maintenance became burdensome and expensive due to the frequent need to replace the untreated, rotten poles.[4]

The Flippen exchange had been founded by its leading citizen, A. G. Harris (who also owned the county's only cider manufacturing business). In 1900, at the age of sixty he sold those businesses and his farm and moved to McDonough where he soon became judge of the Court of Ordinary, an elected office. His office was in effect the governing agency for the entire county for a time. The Mr. Berry who is mentioned in Anna J.'s letter (he will also be mentioned in one of the other Anna's letters) lived near enough to be a subscriber/share holder in the Flippen telephone exchange, and he lived near enough to the Wilsons to know the conditions in the Wilson household. I am assuming the man in question to be Will Berry, who lived just at the end of the road on which the Wilson family farm sat, right at the point where it connected with the road passing through Flippen. Like Judge Harris, though at a later date, Mr. Berry moved to McDonough. Our grandfather, about ten years younger, maintained a friendship with this Mr. Berry throughout the latter's life.

In 1907–1908 Martin had been quite ill—there is no way to know from this letter how long the illness had lasted. (In another letter—this one from Mack Carnes—we learn that the illness had been at a severe stage about November 1907.) As Martin was recovering, sometime in the late winter or early spring before Anna J. wrote, he had apparently expressed disgruntlement that she

---

[4] Morris, *True Southerners*, 90

seemed not to have been attentive enough. In her letter of April 9, she pleads her case: She had sent a card, which he had not acknowledged; she had visited, and he had hardly noted her presence; she assumes his complete disinterest in her ministrations.

Dear Martin,

Your note to hand this A.M. and was read with astonishment. Little did I think you were holding such a feeling toward me for not having been more thoughtful of you in your sickness. I'll give you my reasons: I heard [indecipherable] and again that you were unconscious and phoned to Mr. Berrys (sic) *and learned that it was true. Then I thought what good would a letter do in a case like this—only a nuisance. Then, too, when I went over to see you, you seemed not to notice much and seemed so low I did not think you cared for me, and besides you have one [card] that was sent before yours was returned or else I mailed it. Thinking then that after you had begun improving you would at least answer my card and or let me hear some way. Every line that Mr. John* [probably Martin's oldest brother] *wrote was answered, and I thank him for it all. I am sorry you had such a misfortune, but you will say I need none of your sympathy as you seemed not to appreciate the last. Maybe someday you will see that lots of things were different from what you took them to be. Yes, no doubt there are "<u>others</u>" that wrote you and sympathized with you more than I, to your mind. You will say by their actions they did, and all the blame rests on me. Well, roll it on me. I can bear it. Have had to bear many things that were not pleasant at all and can bear more. Now if I have offended you in such a way without the knowledge of it at the time, don't think I will ever try to be mindful of anything any more. Just take what comes and then make the best of it. They* [who the "they" are there is no way to know] *can see I am indeed sorry and wish for you many happy years and may you never have such indifference shown you by anyone any more as shown by me.*

Hoping that you shall find these explanations sufficient

and that you at some time may realize your indifference but guess it will be at a later date. Too late, possibly for any good — for both of us.

I shall cherish good thoughts of you and think of others [other thoughts?] *only when presented with these remarks.*

She finishes, *I sign again, Anna,* and adds the date, April 9, 1908. It seems to me that a very real hurt weeps its way through these words. They probably signal an end to the friendship between Anna J. and Uncle Martin. Since we do not know her identity, we don't know whether a casual acquaintance with occasional social encounters ensues; if she continued to live in the area, that is likely. Since we know so little of him, there is no way to know whether he lived with regret at his misjudgment of character and intent. One cannot help wondering why he kept the letters, unless they served as a sorrowful reminder that he and she had come to a time "too late, possibly, for any good" to come from attempting to continue a friendship that had been damaged beyond repair.

Chapter Three
"I WOULD BE BETTER SATISFIED TO CONTINUE GOING WITH YOU AS HERETOFORE."
ANNA, RIVERDALE, GEORGIA, 1906

That Martin kept the letters from the other Anna is even harder to fathom, though she does write about her "love" for him and of "going with" him. This Anna, writing from Riverdale, was corresponding with Martin during 1906, as was Anna J. Certainly, one of her letters is from 1906—Anna dates it: "May 8 '06." It is the letter with a missing page or pages. We have identified it as hers from the handwriting. The other letter carries no date beyond "Thursday A.M." It surely was written later than the May letter, and its content would make one suppose that there were no more letters after that one.

Excerpt from Letter of Thursday morning, from Anna of Riverdale

Riverdale is a town in northwest Clayton County. While over

the course of more than a century, Flippen has become a bedroom community, Riverdale has grown to be the very picture of urban sprawl. Located only about twelve miles from downtown Atlanta and just five miles south of Atlanta's Hartsfield-Jackson International Airport—the "busiest in the world"—the city has a population of over fourteen thousand people. Four state highways pass through, and there are four roads of more than four lanes. Some of them are not designated state highways; the lanes are just needed to facilitate the traffic. At the beginning of the twentieth century, Riverdale might have been larger than Flippen, but not by much. The town of the early twentieth century can still be seen off the major thoroughfare passing through (State Route 85); it is located just behind a popular doughnut shop. Our Aunt Miriam's grandfather, C. S. Hemperley, who served at least one term as mayor, owned a general store in the block of buildings that sat along Main Street's raised sidewalk. Part of State Route 139 coincides with this old Main Street, after the state route makes a curve at Church Street before feeding its cars a few hundred yards farther into SR 85, right at the doughnut shop. The sidewalk in front of that block of old buildings (three, sharing common walls, all the buildings now empty) is today at ground level, a by-product of road leveling. Mr. Hemperley's house, which was on Church Street, was in easy walking distance of his store, and the property included gardens, vineyards, chicken coops, and barns.

There were plantations in the area before the Civil War; thirty and forty years later some of them survived as prosperous farms—more survived as struggling concerns. There were also several churches, many of them offering schools to which children might walk from as far away as three or four miles. One school sat so near the Flint River that children had to walk an elevated boardwalk (called "rails" in the account) over the river's back water. Any heavy rain made an acceptable excuse to skip school. Almost as soon as the town began to grow—and two decades before it was incorporated—a two-story building was erected that became its first school. The year was 1890. The building's top floor served the Masons and the Odd Fellows; the bottom floor was the one-room "Seat of Learning." Later a stage and dressing rooms were added to the front of the building—on the outside—for use in days' long exhibitions. Classes would also assemble under some shade trees for special study periods, "all of this done in a very orderly manner," it was reported. "With Mr. Denton [the principal] no one dared be disorderly."[5]

The town's growth dates to 1887 when a railroad connecting Atlanta and Fort Valley (south of Macon) was built. Farmers in the area where Riverdale would soon be established began selling cord wood to the railroad to fire its steam engines, and some enterprisers began off-loading fertilizer to make fertilizer sales the area's first business. There are descriptions years later of children walking to school holding noses closed against the acrid smell. When it became known that the railroad needed land for side tracks, a depot, and housing for its workers, Mr. and Mrs. W. S. Rivers, who owned all the land that would become the town's entire business district, made a donation to the railroad, and Riverdale became a main stop for the railroad. The town named for them was incorporated in 1908. After a brief period of prosperity, "in the early twenties, during the first stage of the depression, the boll weevil came in such numbers that they almost completely destroyed the cotton crop, which . . . was the money crop of this section." The report in *The History of the City of Riverdale* continues: "The loss of shipping and other commodities connected with its [cotton's] growth, also much of the passenger trade, compelled the railroad to discontinue the trains from Atlanta to Fort Valley so the track was taken up and the property sold."[6]

When Anna lived there—while she taught school and boarded, boarding with an uncle's family—the town was enjoying a degree of prosperity. It had much to offer young people. There was a two-story hotel, with a restaurant serving some of the best food in the

---

[5] *History of the City of Riverdale*, 6.
[6] *History of the City of Riverdale*, 14.

area. There were "several swimming pools—just private ponds and dammed streams," reports the history of the city compiled decades later, "but one could boat ride, and swim right on; also croquet and tennis courts, with swings and seats nearby for the spectators."[7] There was a baseball diamond—in some of the town's early decades, the Riverdale team, whatever its league name, was called the "Invincible Huies," with several members from various branches of that family, along with other young athletes, forming its roster. There is no indication that Martin ever played baseball (or was a fan of the game, either), but he might well have learned to play tennis in company of Anna of Riverdale.

The late reader picking up Anna's letter today knows that she is entering an ongoing saga between Anna and Martin and feels Anna's distress soon enough to realize that the writer has omitted a key word from her very first sentence.

Riverdale, Ga.
May 8, '06

Dear Martin,
*You will no doubt [**not**] be thinking of me this morning, or anything that pertains to my happiness from the way you seem to take what I told you when I was with you last. I did not mean to hurt your feelings or to say anything that would make you think I did not care for you, but, as I told you to simply try my own self and test my love for you by an absence of I did not know how long. I think I would be better satisfied to continue going with you as heretofore, but guess maybe your feelings are so wounded you will have no feeling for mine. I did not doubt a word you said and would not have acted so bad if [it had] not been for my doubts about myself and am fully satisfied now, and hope you are not wounded so badly as I fear.*
Did you get the photo? I mailed it in the first mail box this side of the bridge west of Mr. Berry's, and don't know whether I though[t] to leave the flag up or not. If I didn't It (sic) is there

---

[7] *History of the City of Riverdale*, 9.

> yet. I am here at Uncle Joe's don't know just how long I shall remain though Something (sic) like a week I guess. I am not going to S. C. [South Carolina] until the middle of June, if then, and will only be gone two weeks. Then come back here for my school. L. E. has come home on account of her mother's illness and will go back for the children in June and I will join her in Atlanta.
>
> I am not having such an enjoyable time since I came this time, haven't been well at all since I have been here, but am feeling better this morning. Now, Martin, I hope you are not offended with me for what I did as I told you it wasn't anything you had or hadn't done but for the reason I gave you. If you like it will suit me al[right] . . .

And there ends what we have of this letter. One wonders what came next. I assume that I have added the correct ending for the word continued on the next page and that Anna was ready, perhaps, to receive his company again. Clearly, they have been "going" together. Reading between the lines, one imagines that he has pressed his suit, and that she has doubts, even if she does write about testing her "love" and not his. She worries that she has "wounded" his feelings; she seems to want time and distance and some busyness of life to give them space to sort things out.

The mention of the mailbox near Mr. Berry's raises questions. How does she know Mr. Berry? Her knowing him (and the location of his house) suggests that she is from Flippen (in that case the two Annas may, in fact, be the same young woman), or from Stockbridge, or from the farming community where Martin and Mr. Berry live. The letter's date, May 8, does not correspond to the beginning of a school term, but rather to its end, or an approaching end. The letter suggests that she had had a longer time away from Uncle Joe's (maybe the Christmas break), but, since coming back "this time," she has been unwell. She outlines plans for the summer—a visit to South Carolina, some time in Atlanta. None of these plans involves him. She has explained to him that she is willing to go on as before, but the whole tone of the letter bespeaks a "tired of it all" attitude. Nevertheless, the relationship does continue.

There is no way to know when she writes the next letter. The heading says Riverdale, but it carries no date beyond "Thursday A. M." He had visited the evening before—a midweek visit. Was there anything unusual in that? Had there been a church service that prompted the topic of their last conversation? Were midweek prayer meetings the norm at that time? Is the letter written and posted so early in the morning that she gave herself no time to reconsider? What is her mood when she pens it? Regret, so that its tone is remorseful? Or anger, so that its tone is a barely controlled sarcasm?

Riverdale, Ga
Thursday A. M.

Dear Martin,

Since last night I can think of nothing but the words you spoke to me about my Christian experience. I am glad now that you took such a bold idea and let me know your thoughts on that line. Having seen my life so impure and ungodly, you could not bear for me to approach you on the same. I thought I was living right but having so impressed you for the length of time that we have associated with each other otherwise, all I can do now is ask your forgiveness for such a careless and neglectful example and pray for new light and to be purer, better, and a nobler girl in the future. If my light has been so dim, I must thank you for telling me of it and will say no more about your condition, so long as mine is as it seems. And by God's grace lead a different life in the future.

Hoping someday to be the girl I always wished to be and that God in his all-wise eye will so direct me that my life will be a living testimony, leading others to the feet of the meek and lowly Jesus and to so live that I will be above reproach.

The same
Anna

What do you do with such a letter if your intent in reading the letters has been to discover the man to whom they were written? Who is he at this point in his life? Did he, too, remain ever the same? Anna J., in her last letter, asks his forgiveness for any lapse in care she might have shown him in his illness, when it seemed to be he who had been judgmental, he who should have been asking for forgiveness. And now Anna, always "the same," suffers at his hand a similar judgmentalism. Perhaps, as she implies, whatever he had said has awakened her to some needed self-examination. But what of him? Did he keep the letter, which should have broken his heart, so that he might reread the burden her words could have placed on him: "You could not bear for me to approach you on the same"—the nature of his own life: was it, too, "impure and ungodly"? "[I] will say no more about your condition, so long as mine is as it seems," she adds. There is, also, a challenge: Can he pray the same prayer—"that God in his all-wise eye will so direct [him] that [his] life will be a living testimony, leading others to the feet of the meek and lowly Jesus"?

Does this time in his life mark a turning point? The timing is an unsure thing in a letter bearing no date. For the next letter, a rather long one—this one from a male friend—we have a date, a life circumstance, and a clear challenge for a change in his life. Before we get to that letter, I want to set Martin among a people and in a place that had formed him to this point in his life.

The Anna Letters

Dates	Correspondent
January 1, 1906 (certain)	Anna J. (from Flippen, certain)
May 8, 1906 (certain)	Anna (from Riverdale, certain)
Thursday, the 10th. May 10, 1906 (month and year uncertain) October 10, 1907 (less likely)	Anna (from Flippen, certain)
The "Thursday A.M." letter	Anna (from Riverdale, certain)
No mention of Martin's illness, so it probably was written before he fell ill—between fall of 1906 and fall of 1907.	
Martin's illness: fall 1907–spring 1908	
April 9, 1908 (certain)	Anna (from Flippen, certain)

The letters of January 1, 1906, (date certain) and May 10, 1906, (date assigned) read as if the friendship is new. Both are from Flippen.

The letter from Riverdale of May 8, 1906, (date certain) reads as if the friendship is a long-standing one, with this Anna using her residence in Riverdale as a period of "testing" the nature of the friendship. The "Thursday A.M." letter (date uncertain) marks the end of that friendship.

The April 9, 1908, letter from Flippen marks the end of a friendship also, and I find it unlikely that the same woman would have written two such letters.

Chapter Four
"I DESIRE THAT MY BROTHER MARTIN ALONZO WILSON BE PAID THE SUM OF FIVE DOLLARS ... OUT OF MY ESTATE." MARTIN'S FAMILY

Martin's roots were deep in Henry County, which had been founded in 1821 after the Treaty of Indian Springs between the United States and the Creek (Muskogee) Indians. Martin's great-grandfather, Joshua Wilson, an illiterate farmer who had to sign his 1847 will with an X, described the property he bequeathed in that will as a "plantation." The property, at something more than five hundred acres, was not nearly so large as popular imagination holds a plantation to have been, but it was large enough to fit the category. Joshua's son, the first John Thomas Wilson, also bequeathed a "plantation" in a will that was also marked with an X. It would not be unheard of for a young woman who named herself a teacher in the census record, as Sophronia Susan Turner did, to marry a man of no schooling, but I imagine for the second John Thomas, her bridegroom, at least some basic literacy. Sophronia and the second John Thomas are the couple who became parents to our grandfather, to Uncle Martin, to four other sons, and to Aunt Betty.

John Thomas predeceased his wife. He is not buried, however, beside her in the Noah's Ark cemetery where she left a hexagonal spire of a grave marker, which, because it is engraved "Susan Wilson," lets the world know how much she disliked having been named Sophronia. (The two initials, with the *W*, are engraved on the footstone—*SSW*.) John Thomas's body is buried in the family's cemetery on their farm, where he died in the late 1890s. Apparently, the family was not allowed to inter him in the churchyard because he died of some sort of plague—that is the tale of family lore. It is probably for that reason also—the suddenness of his demise—that he died intestate.

John Thomas and Sophronia named their firstborn John Thomas, after his father and grandfather. The third John Thomas was married—rather late in life—to a woman still of childbearing years, though older than most first-time married women. However, the couple never had children. The wife, our Aunt Eunice, had two sisters who never married (the oldest sister did marry) and two mentally challenged younger brothers for whom the unmarried sisters cared all their lives. It would be presumptuous to think that Uncle John and Aunt Eunice were childless by choice, though that might have been the case. The youngest brother in Aunt Eunice's family was perfectly normal. He—P. K. Dixon—served Clayton County so many years as commission chairman that today's government complex includes an annex bearing his name.

John Thomas and Sophronia's second son was Bunard Starr, who was called Bun. He was the first of the children to die, decades earlier than any of his siblings, only forty-six years old, unmarried. There is a picture of him in a rather stiff and formal pose—if he were younger, one would suppose it to be a school photograph, and perhaps it is. The photograph might also suggest a job, such as bank teller or store clerk, rather than farming, but he reports himself to be a farmer in 1920, though he owns only small properties. There is a copy of Bun's holographic will, dated October 20, 1920; he died on March 30, 1921, so I will assume that he was in ill health, and might have been for some time, and that he was diligent about making final arrangements:

> Georgia. Clayton Co. [the will reads]. I Bunard Starr Wilson of the County and State aforesaid being of

sound and disposing mind and memory do hereby make this my last will and testament expressly revoking and annulling any and all other heretofore made by me.

Item 1. I desire that my body to buried in a Christian like manner suitable to my circumstances.

Item 2. I desire that my Executor hereinafter named proceed to pay all my just debts as rapidly as possible.

Item 3. I give to my Sister Elizabeth Arddella [spelled this way in this instance; spelled differently later in the same document] Wilson all that track (*sic*) and parcel of land lying and being in the Sixth land District of Clayton County, Georgia, and consisting of thirty four (34) acres and being part of the Mrs. Jim Cox Estate and part of Land lot No. 35 and bounded as follows on the North (*sic*) by land of Homer Floyd and E. H. Fife, on the West (*sic*) by land of M. F. Holloway, on the North (*sic*) by A. M. Wilson, on the East (sic) by B. S. Wilson, Et. al. this [indecipherable] of land deeded to J. T. Wilson by J. M Cox Et. Al. Nov. 21, 1905.

Item 4. I give to my brother Wm. Chas. Wilson my interest in two (2) acres of land[,] dwelling[,] farm[,] together with all and Singular (*sic*) the [indecipherable] and appurtenances thereto in any wise belonging thereto the same being deeded to B. S. Wilson, Et.al. No[v]. 21, 1908 by [indecipherable].

Item 5. I desire that my brother John Thomas Wilson be paid the Sum (*sic*) of five dollars in money out of my Estate (*sic*).

Item 6. I desire that my brother Martin Alonzo Wilson be paid the Sum of five dollars in money out of my Estate.

Item 7. I desire that my brother Wiley Sims Wilson be paid the Sum of five dollars in money out of my Estate.

Item 8. I desire that my brother Miles Turner

Wilson be paid the Sum of five dollars in money out of my Estate.

Item 9. I desire that the remainder of my property that I should die seized with real[,] personal[,] and mixed be Equally (*sic*) divided between my Sister (*sic*) Elizabeth Ardella Wilson and my brother Wm. Chas. Wilson.

Item 10. I hereby appoint as Executor of this my Will (*sic*) my brother John Thomas Wilson.

In testimony Whereof (*sic*) I hereunto set my hand this the [not included] day of Oct. 1920.

Sign[ed] and published by Bunard Starr Wilson as his last will and testament in the presence of the [indecipherable] hereto as Witnesses (*sic*) at the instance and request of said testator and in the presence of Each (*sic*) other. This the 20th of Oct. 1920.

B. S. Wilson

Witness

J. B. Pulliam

C. D. Dickson

B. L. Walden

Photograph of Uncle Bun (date unknown) superimposed on his holographic will (1920)

The bequests of five dollars "in money" probably meant five dollar gold pieces, indicating not much faith that paper money would hold its value. These small bequests most likely were intended to forestall any challenge to the will, though a challenge was unlikely to have been forthcoming. The amount can be seen as an indication that no one in the family was particularly well off. Even the acreage Bun owned was decidedly modest. Our mother was not yet two years old when Bun died. Of course, she never knew this uncle; that is probably why we have no stories of his life and are limited to locating his grave and tombstone in Noah's Ark cemetery, acknowledging, "There lies our Uncle Bun, under that marker." The marker is one he shares with Martin, who died more than thirty years later.

Wiley Sims and Nola Odessa Hemperley Wilson on their Wedding Day, March 11, 1908

Our grandfather, Wiley Sims Wilson, was born two years after Martin. In the years when Martin was corresponding with the friends whose letters are gathered here, Wiley was farming and raising a family with Nola Odessa Hemperley, whom he married in 1908. The son born to them in 1917, the last year of Martin's letters, was the fifth of their nine children. His name was Frank Sims, the Sims, of course, from his father. Frank was killed just days before the Battle of the Bulge, a few miles from the German border, on December 14, 1944. We have his letters, too—they form the core of a longer memoir. In his letters, he often mentions having heard from Uncle Martin.

The oldest of Frank's siblings were two sisters, Maurene and Bessie, then there was a brother, J. T., and another sister, Willie. The *J* in J. T. stands for James, not John; our grandparents, if they had thought of it at all, might have decided to leave the name John for Uncle John to give to the son he never had. Nola's father and her brother were both James Beauregards. Apparently, their grandfather was serving under General P. G. T. Beauregard during the Civil War at the time of their father's birth. Uncle Jim had no son to carry the name on, but J. T.'s *James* was probably given in honor of his mother's father and her brother.

No one ever spoke, as far as I know, of any reason for the only sister in the family, two years younger than Wiley, never to have married. How we would like to have found Aunt Betty's letters—there must have been some. Not from beaux, perhaps (though that too), but from friends and aunts and uncles and cousins, and from siblings, also, when they were away. When Frank was killed, there was a letter to Martin and Betty from their aunt Nellie J. Turner in Texas expressing her condolences. The aunt must have been corresponding with them regularly. And if people wrote to one another from towns so near as Flippen and Riverdale, surely there were letters from those places, too, as well as from faraway Texas, addressed to Betty. She died more than fifteen years after Martin did; it is she who kept the Martin letters for us to find. What did she do with her own?

She was a quiet and hardworking woman, keeping house and working in barnyard, chicken yard, and garden—and probably slopping the hogs, too. Her chores must have been endless. The cooking, for which she was locally well-known—and in the family down through the years, much appreciated—was done in a cookhouse in the middle of the back yard, at least in the summer, the cookhouse under the same roof as the smokehouse. The cookhouse memory is from my brother, Michael, who was born the same year Martin died. I recall the outdoor cookhouse not at all.

Mike would have known the building from his explorations about the property with cousins about his age whose father, Raymond, acquired it after Martin's death. Little boy Mike's memory might be more accurate than mine, however, for Aunt Betty continued to live, with her youngest brother, Charlie, in the hilltop house for a few years after Martin's death, and Mike would have known the place then--in the years when I was in my teens and paying the house and its occupants scant attention.

When Betty did cook in the smokehouse shed, maybe she rose early to build a fire in the cook stove, or maybe Martin—or Charlie— did that, or perhaps they banked it. The reason for the outdoor kitchen's location was to keep the house from becoming overheated as much as to prevent a cooking fire from burning it down. There was also a wood-burning stove in the indoor kitchen (this memory is mine), and meals were served there or in the adjacent dining room. If cooking was done in that kitchen only in winter months, then the fire was most welcome for the warmth it would bring.

Whether the other rooms in that big drafty house, which was set on piers, had fireplaces or heating stoves set on hearths in front of closed-off fireplaces, I don't recall. The setting on stone piers (field rocks they were, the interior piers) left welcome play space beneath the house, ideal for nieces and nephews, especially during summertime visits. We could spend hours in that cool space, making hiding places or just crawling around and in and out. The favorite thing to do was to sing the doodle bugs out: "Doodle bug, doodle bug, won't you come home?" Our digging at them with short sticks made a sure answer to the invitation. Once the bug came out, it curled itself into a neat little ball. What did we do with it then? Did we just toss it aside to find its way back underground?

There was cleaning, of course, for Betty to do, no matter the season—bedding to change and rugs to beat, floors to sweep and to mop and wax. And, in their household, as in every farm household, those tasks associated with the products of the hard-worked farm: milking and churning; planting, hoeing, harvesting, and canning; berrying and pie- and jam-making. Martin might wear store-bought overalls and suits; she sewed her own clothes, and, in our day, she often wore, on weekdays, two dresses, letting one, maybe it was a shift of sorts, serve as undergarment. Outdoors she always wore a sunbonnet, and a tidier, prettier hat to church. For church, she must have donned a petticoat, too, and dainty gloves to cover the work-worn hands. There was the laundry on washdays, with heavy pots of water to heat and clothes to wring out by hand or with the help of a scrub board and hang on lines to dry. Then, of course, those same clothes must be ironed with the iron heated on stove top.

She lost two sisters-in-law, mothers to children she then had to help rear. Wiley's Nola died in 1929, when our mother, Zelma—she was called Jule—was ten. She and her three youngest siblings, Raymond, Doris, and Leon, though they never lived with Martin and Betty, fell to Betty's motherly attention. We know from our mother that it was hardly appreciated. Auntie Betty cut hair with a bowl to guide her shaping, and the cut was ugly; she pinched arms to keep children quiet and attentive in church; and she was a strict taskmaster, setting a determined working pace.

The brother four years younger than Betty was one of the four siblings who did marry. Miles Turner was called by his mother's maiden name. On the last day of 1906—he was all of twenty-one—Turner married Jessie B. Roberts; their oldest child was born in 1908. He was named Weyman R. (for Roberts), but he was called, surely in his childhood, as throughout his life, Buck or Buster. Two daughters were born after Buck—Johnnie Mae in 1912 and Grace in 1915, and then Jessie died in 1919. Turner was able to manage his role as a single father for some years, but by 1930, when the two older children were young marrieds and starting families of their own, the younger daughter, Grace (Elizabeth Grace), was living with Uncle Martin and Aunt Betty, and Turner was keeping company with an unsuitable woman, whom he claimed to have married.

Charlie, the youngest Wilson brother, we have already met, briefly. Charlie did marry, and he became father to a daughter who was named for Aunt Betty—Climmie Elizabeth. (There are lots of Elizabeths in our family—thankfully, no Sophronias.) How long his marriage to Climmie's mother, Belle, lasted I don't know. There was a divorce—an absolutely unheard thing in families such as ours in those so-young years of the twentieth century, therefore never spoken of. So, we don't know the reason for it. I sometimes imagined that Uncle Charlie had been a drinker, but I don't think I ever heard anybody say that. I probably created that story in my mind to balance the religiosity the older Charlie exhibited, thinking it romantic to give him a recognizable problem and completely unaware, if he had suffered from it, how devastating a disease alcoholism is and how difficult to recover from. Climmie's mother remarried, and Climmie had a half-sister, whom I never met, as far as I know, though I was for a time close to Climmie's only daughter, Merle, a cousin lucky enough to live in Atlanta where her mother had grown to adulthood.

After the divorce, Charlie never married again. He lived alone on some farm he was renting either in Clayton or in Henry County—census records show him at a different address from any of his siblings, though always in, or near, the Noah's Ark community. After living for a time with Martin and Betty—and with Betty after Martin's death (one of my younger sisters calls the old house "Uncle Charlie's house")— sometime in the 1950s, Charlie had a house built in Stockbridge, near the Holiness Church that he had come to support wholeheartedly, and Aunt Betty moved there with him. She, however, suffered declining health and spent her last years in a nursing home, dying in 1968, two days after our grandfather, and five years earlier than Charlie.

Betty's and Charlie's graves are together; they share a common tombstone. To Betty's left, our grandfather lies interred beneath a stone he, of course, shares with Nola, who had predeceased him by four decades. All the Wilson siblings are buried in the cemetery at Noah's Ark Church (John Thomas III lies in the Dixon plot), for that church was the center of their community's life, and thus a center for their lives, too.

Chapter Five
"It was the prayers . . . at old Noah's Ark that reached God." Martin's Church and Community

We have already noted Martin's illness late in the fall of 1907 and the slow recovery that lasted into the spring of 1908. It distressed family, friends, and neighbors. Naturally, throughout the illness and the months of recovery, his church was much in prayer for him, as the quote from the friend who writes about it a year later reminds him. Noah's Ark Church dates to 1852; from its founding it was a Methodist church (a Methodist Episcopal Church, South, until 1939). It is today independent and non-denominational. The road on which it sits is Noah's Ark Road, but, with changes over time, more than a century and a half later, one can hardly speak of a Noah's Ark community, except in the narrow sense of the church's active and affiliated memberships. Today there are at least four churches in the area identified as the historic Noah's Ark community, but the first of them appeared only in the 1960s. In succeeding decades, as subdivisions replaced farms and as the new churches were planted, residents came more and more to identify with Jonesboro or with Stockbridge, the nearest towns, rather than with Noah's Ark, unless they happened to be members of Noah's Ark Church, and the community lost its character. But, for Martin's generation, church and community were one.

On the plot of ground where the church sits there had been an earlier church, Mt. Pleasant, meeting at the site of an academy.

Dorothea Whitaker McAlvin

When the academy ceased operation in 1849, so did the church, and another church, Ebenezar (this is the spelling that we have in the sources), that had been meeting somewhere to the east of Mt. Pleasant, became interested in the property. The congregation purchased the five-acre plot at a sheriff's sale for twenty-five dollars. Apparently, trustees from the two churches acted together to organize the new church. The trustees—David Dailey, Eli Carnes, Samuel Lee, William L. Campbell, and William C. Lee—soon enough constructed a sanctuary. The old academy was not revived, though some time later a public elementary school did meet at the church.

The church had been chartered in Henry County, but in 1858 the land on which it sits became part of the newly created Clayton County, and the church has a Jonesboro address. The present sanctuary, smaller than the original, perhaps because it had no need for the separate section for slaves that the original had, was built and furnished in 1889 at a cost of $1,400. Two explanations have been offered for the church's name: One holds that the name honors a pastor, a Noah Smith, who cannot be found in the records. The other claims that someone remarked that the new building looked like an ark. This conjecture is less likely because the name predates the construction of the second sanctuary.

That ark of a sanctuary was a one-room structure, with a high-pitched roof. Its exterior was clapboard, always painted white; the interior walls, and the lofty ceiling, too, were white planking. At window-sill height, there was dark tongue-in-groove wainscot, topped with rounded molding, that ran the perimeter of the space. A relatively ornate lectern—dark walnut—stood centered between the windows on the back, the northern, wall. The pulpit area was two concentric half circles. On the upper level stood the lectern; the lower supported the altar rail—also dark walnut, but not ornate. The communion table sat inside the rail and just in front of the lectern.

The church was heated by a pot-bellied stove as late as the 1940s and early 1950s and cooled through lovely, long windows in the years before air conditioning. The windows, of course, admitted flies and wasps along with the welcome breeze. And over their sills, the snuff-dippers, like our grandfather—who, when in attendance, claimed a regular window-side seat—could aim their spittle. Sunday school classes met in different corners of that one room. As late as the mid-1960s, the building still had two front entrances, signaling its erection in the days when men and women entered through different doors. The rare wedding party (mine among them) could process down one aisle and recess out the other. The groom awaited the beginning of the processional at a side entrance, even as the bees of a summer's day might have been tormenting him and his attendants.

Some of the names that we find among the church's original trustees continue down through the generations—Carnes, Campbell, Lee; other names that continue in residence include those we find in Uncle Bun's will—Wilson, of course, and Floyd, and Holloway, all owning property adjacent to the property he was bequeathing. The Fife name Bun gives as one of those property owners disappeared from our ken, and the Coxes who had sold land as part of settling an estate either died off or moved away. On the census page with the Wilsons in 1920, there are these names: Tomlin, Johnson, Gilbert. (And a state senator named Johnson had been holder of the church's first deed.) There are names of Black families on those census pages, also, for this farming community depended on them. If the Black families didn't own their own farms, they worked the land as tenants on whatever share agreement or rental contract owner and tenant devised, or they worked as hired hands. One Black farmer reported himself to be an "employer"—the usual designation for a farmer/owner with renters or sharecroppers working for and with him. Women in these families, in addition to their own house and field work, found employment with the White families, but mostly, I think, of an occasional nature: spring cleaning, unusually large washdays, nursing the sick or caring for new babies, and catering big events. Some families might have hired them as housekeepers, cooks, or nursemaids, but Noah's Ark's White households were for the most part self-maintained.

Except for working together in the fields, particularly at cotton picking time, residents in the community lived segregated lives. The church was a Whites-only congregation though no one had to make that a policy statement: it just was. Black and White social lives intersected only at the point where one family might require another family's assistance—the White family taking along a cook or nursemaid at camp meeting time for example, or the Black family seeking transportation to town for some critical need. The men might hunt together, and when one farmer had a big task to do—say, a hog killing—lots of neighbors, White and Black, might show up. I have no stories about the many moonshine stills, remains of which my brother was finding along the creeks as he tramped the woods in his boyhood. Our grandfather might have been associated with them, but of other folk, White or Black, we heard no speculation.

During the Great Depression decade, when every farmer found it difficult to continue and few could provide employment to others, many of the Black families moved away, so that by the fifties, there were few still living in the community. A Black family surnamed Mann appeared in an early census; some members of that family still lived in or near Noah's Ark in our youth. There was a "Dade" Mann among them. Of course, to children that sounded like Dead Man, and I don't know that we ever wanted to look in his direction if anyone pointed him out. He was a big, muscular man, I am told, just the sort of man you would hire for digging a septic tank. My brother, Mike, remembers that our father hired him for that job, and that he, a tyke of three, fell into the pit or onto the dirt that had been dug out. "Why, you little turd," one of the men, our father or the "Dead Man," called him, and the adults laughed—in relief, I'm sure, at his safe recovery.

Black children were as likely as White children to be able to read and write in the early years of the twentieth century, so they were all getting a minimum of schooling somewhere. The *History of the City of Riverdale* provides a list of schools for the Black children in that area. The Noah's Ark Public School was in session as late as 1924; the school, which went through at least the seventh grade, accommodated the White children in the Clayton County section of the community. Children who lived in Henry County had no school so near to them. The school my mother's oldest siblings attended, which was also the one she entered for her first year (1925), was too far from their house for a walk, but mule and wagon got them there. That school was located at a great distance from any town, but it served as a center for at least two rural communities, Dutchtown having perhaps a clearer geographic claim than Noah's Ark. It is interesting to note that some children in White families who lived in the area in the first decades of the twentieth century were reported to be able to read, but not able to write.

Atlanta was easily accessible to the residents of Noah's Ark—by way of roads yet unpaved and by railway. Black families as well as White probably had kinfolk in the city, so that news of any major event could reach the community as it was happening—especially if the event stretched out over several days, as did the Race Riot of 1906.

Chapter Six
"THE SLAUGHTER OF THE INNOCENT DOES DRIVE AWAY CITIZENS." ATLANTA, 1906

There is one letter in this small collection that seems the type that would ordinarily be thrown away. It contains the receipt for a purchase, and perhaps the receipt should have been kept—for a time. But the fact that the letter which had enclosed the receipt was also kept is probably just a happenstance. Surely, it held little value to Martin or to Betty, if she ever read or reread the letters that she saved. The letter does, however, open a passage through which we can examine some details of the Atlanta Race Riot of 1906. Martin has promised one M. S. McMullen, of Jonesboro—her name was Mattie, according to a note someone added to the envelope—that he would send a money order for a subscription to *The Atlanta Georgian and Evening News*; when she receives the money order, she sends the receipt—and a thank you note. The receipt shows how small Georgia's capital city was in 1908:

> In case of irregular delivery, phone Bell 8000.
> Received $4.50 from M. A. Wilson, Stockbridge GA.

The Atlanta Georgian was a daily—an afternoon issue. It was a new paper in Atlanta, dating only to 1905. It had begun in reformer mode, criticizing saloons and the convict labor system. But in the next year it joined the other Atlanta papers in a campaign of gross malfeasance that ended in the race riot. Like any such event, the Atlanta Race Riot had multiple causes[8]:

- The movement of Black people into the city in recent decades, their numbers quadrupling from an 1880 baseline—an increase two times greater than the increase among Whites.
- Competition among White and Black workers for jobs.
- Resentment on the part of some Whites at the success of Atlanta's Black elite business and professional class.
- The anti-saloon league's effort to close bars which depicted the bars as "dens of iniquity," of course, but also as places where the two races might mingle, and Black men ogle at paintings of naked White women.

The 1906 gubernatorial race provided the context. In Georgia, as in other states of the old Confederacy, the Democratic Party at the time was all-White. Black people were Republican—the party of Lincoln the Emancipator, and of the Reconstruction Republicans who had secured the vote for adult Black men in the adoption of the Fifteenth Amendment to the Constitution. That vote the White Democrats had ever afterward tried to take away. The loser of the Democratic Party's primary election, Clark Howell, made Black disfranchisement the central issue of his campaign, but the eventual winner, Hoke Smith, not to be outdone, proved to be as much a White supremacist as the loser. The disfranchisement cause, press coverage of it, and newspaper

---

[8] Gregory Mixon and Clifford Kuhn, "Atlanta Race Riot of 1906." *New Georgia Encyclopedia*, 08/27/2020. See also Gary Pomerantz, *Where Peachtree Meets Sweet Auburn. A Saga of Race and Family.* (New York: Simon and Schuster, 1996), 72-77, and Georgia Public Television. Georgia Stories, Cliff Kuhn and Carole Merritt, "The Race Riot of 1906," gpb.org.

editorials in support of it contributed to a highly charged anti-Black atmosphere among Atlanta's White residents. It didn't help that a play, *The Clansman*, source for the D. W. Griffith movie *Birth of a Nation*, was being staged that summer in Atlanta; it had not been allowed to open in Montgomery, Alabama, or in Macon, Georgia.

Still, the rioting had to have an immediate cause. The primary was decided in August and the riots started weeks later, toward the end of September. The general election was still to come—in October. Although its outcome had already been decided in the primary voting, electioneering was still a topical issue for the newspapers. There were four of them. (This discussion leaves out the Black-owned *The Atlanta Independent*, which had published vigorous rebuttals to the political reporting as well as the racist editorializing found in the other papers.) *The Atlanta Journal*, of which Hoke Smith, by profession an attorney, had been part owner, and the *Atlanta Constitution*, which Clark Howell published, were the two powerhouses. Two smaller circulation papers, *The Atlanta Georgian* and *The Evening News*, had been publishing lurid anti-Black stories throughout the year. Now the larger papers, one a morning edition (the *Constitution*), the other an evening edition (the *Journal*), joined them in sensationalizing any story of Black crime and vice, especially stories—none ever substantiated, though a few indictments were handed down—of Black assaults against White women.

On the afternoon of Saturday, September 22, newsboys hit the streets, hawking papers with alarming headlines: "Extra! Extra!" And the reports ranged from a Black man's kissing the hand of a White girl, to a "mulatto" man's insulting a White girl, to the account of a third assault on White women by the same "Negro brute." In the early evening, groups of White men along the saloon-lined streets, "liquored up," began to form themselves into a mob, or into several mobs. They entered the saloons, pulling Black men out, beating them up, stabbing them. If any Black business was open (the most noted barber shop had closed for the day), they entered, attacked, and killed (all the barbers in one shop that had not closed). They pulled men off streetcars and pummeled them to death. There is an account of at least one body hanging from a lamppost. Mayor James G. Woodward called for order—in a speech foreshadowing the speeches to come in Atlanta's more recent history: "The honor of Atlanta *before the world* is in your hands"⁹ (emphasis added). He was shouted down, with cries of "Nigger lover." He was, in fact, as much a racist as any other of the city's—and the state's—establishment leaders. On September 25, the *New York* Times quoted the mayor in its story of the riot. "The best way to prevent a race riot depends entirely upon the cause. If your inquiry has anything to do with the present situation in Atlanta[,] then I would say the only remedy is to remove the cause. As long as the black brutes assault our white women just so long will they be unceremoniously dealt with."[10]

When Woodward called in the police and fire departments to do what they could to restore order, they turned hoses first on the White mob. The scene became more chaotic, however, as Black men fighting for their lives used whatever weapons they could find, and the hoses were turned on them all. Someone sketched the scene, and the visual became the cover of the October 7 issue of *Le Petit Journal*, a magazine published in Paris.

At first, policemen and firemen did what they could to restore order, then some joined the attackers. About midnight Governor Joseph M. Terrell sent in the state militia, but it was only with the coming of rain in the early morning hours that calm was restored. On Sunday, the state militia was able to maintain order, but for the next several nights, rioting continued. Hotels and restaurants

---

[9] Pomerantz, *Where Peachtree Meets Sweet Auburn*, 74.
[10] "Atlanta Race Riot of 1906," Wikipedia.org.http://enwikipedia.org/wiki/1906-Atlanta-race-riot. The Wikipedia entry on the riot I first accessed on May 5, 2020; at that time the mayor's statement was in an endnote. The article did state that since 2006, the centennial anniversary of the riot, the Georgia Department of Education has mandated teaching about the riot in its social studies curriculum. When I last accessed the entry--on August 12, 2021—the mayor's quote was incorporated into the body of the article.

locked their service staffs in, keeping them safe, and families who had Black servants did the same. Black families, and White, too, armed themselves. On Monday, police followed a White mob into Brownsville, a Black residential area where residents had armed themselves for self-protection. One policeman was killed, with a conviction of manslaughter handed down against a Brownsville resident.[11] W. E. B. DuBois, professor at Atlanta University, was on a research assignment in Alabama; he hurried home to wife and child and brought into the house a newly purchased shotgun to protect them. DuBois swore later that he would have used it if his home or the university's campus had been threatened. Margaret Mitchell's father had no gun but guarded his front door with an ax.

In the weeks after the violence subsided, there was an inquiry by an all-White commission. The inquiry results read like a lament:[12]

1. *Among the victims of the mob, there was not a single vagrant.*
2. *They were earning wages in useful work up to the time of the riot.*
3. *They were supporting themselves and their families or dependent relatives.*
4. *Most of the dead left small children and widows, mothers or sisters, with practically no means and very small earning capacity.*
5. *The wounded lost from one to eight weeks' time, at 50 cents to $4.00 a day each.*
6. *About seventy persons were wounded and among these*

---

[11]Dewar, Sheila. "100 Years Later, a Painful Episode is Observed at Last," *The New York Times*, September 24, 2006. https://www.nytimes.com/2006/09/24/us/24riot.html. Accessed May 15, 2020. The policeman's name was James Heard. Alexander Walker served a prison term for killing Heard. A Walker grand-daughter is quoted in the article saying, "Papa didn't take no mess."

[12]Ray Stannard Baker, "A Race Riot, and After." *The American Magazine*. LXVIII, No. 6, April 1907, in digitalbabel.hathitrust.org. Accessed May 15, 2020.

> there was an immense amount of suffering. In some cases, it was prolonged and excruciating pain.
> 7. Many of the wounded are disfigured and several are permanently disabled.
> 8. Most of them were in humble circumstances, but they were honest, industrious and law-abiding citizens and useful members of society.
>
> . . .
>
> 11. Wild rumors of a larger number killed have no foundation that we can discover. As the city was paying for funeral expenses of victims and relief was given their families, they had every reason to make known their loss.
>
> . . .
>
> 14. Although less than three months have passed since the riot, events have already demonstrated that the slaughter of the innocent does not deter the criminal class from committing more crime. Rape and murder have been committed in the city and suburbs during that time.
> 15. The slaughter of the innocent does drive away good citizens. From one small neighborhood twenty-five families are gone. A great many of them were buying homes on the installment plan.
> 16. The crimes of the mob include robbery as well as murder. In a number of cases the property of the innocent and unoffending people was taken. Furniture was destroyed, small shops were looted, windows were smashed, trunks were burst open, money was taken from the small hoard . . .

Historians tell us that White Atlanta kept no memory of this event; Black Atlanta, certainly within the families that were resident at the time, did keep memory of "the slaughter of the innocent." One of the offending papers, *The Evening News*, suffered enough loss in readership that it was easy for the *Georgian* to buy it out the next year. (It is *The Atlanta Georgian and Evening News* to which Martin is subscribing.) In 1912, the *Georgian* was bought by the Hearst chain; it won some awards for excellence in journalism, but it published mostly in the "yellow" vein. James M. Cox bought the Georgian in 1939, when he bought The Atlanta Journal, and quit publication of the Georgian in that same year.

Martin's Subscription

I can find no account of the impact of the Atlanta Race Riots on the Noah's Ark community or its residents. The Wilsons were probably regular subscribers to the local papers, which printed weekly columns reporting news from their community, as well as news from all of the other communities in the area. If this is the first instance of any family member's subscribing to an Atlanta paper, this one was no worse—or only marginally worse—than were the major papers when it came to coverage of political, racial, and social issues.

Martin's decision to take a year's subscription does not necessarily reflect any particular interest in state politics or in national or global affairs. It appears from the letter that Mattie McMullen sent along with his receipt that it was the young woman's easy charm that had led him to purchase his subscription. (I am making no spelling or grammar corrections to her letter.)

Jonesboro Ga
Nov- 23 - 08

Mr. Martin:
   Received P. O. Order this A. M. For Georgian and New's. That amount was all <u>OK. Many Many thank's</u> for your kindness in helping me out would also be glad to have you clip all coupon's especially that one that count's 50 vote's in

> *today's paper If you will send them all in to me I will fill out and mail same.*
>
> *Sure I cant expect to win the capital prize but hope to make a <u>very good race</u>. I have had fine luck this week.*

The capital prize in the contest was a house in West Atlanta, valued at $5,000. Second prize was a touring car; third prize, $1,000 in gold. There were additional prizes, beyond these. The metro Atlanta area was divided into fifteen districts, and there would be winners in each district. The lesser prizes included a land lot, valued at $200; a set of furniture; an electric or gas range, together with an electric or gas iron smoother (an iron for ironing clothes is my best guess). Subscribers were supposed to fill out a form, naming the person who had sold them the subscription. If the subscriber were the first person to nominate an eventual winner, the subscriber would win a $200 prize.[13] But Mattie isn't leaving it up to Martin to complete the form; she instructs him to send it to her so that she could forward it to the paper.

Mattie adds to the letter's content:

> *Say who was the man you had the letter from? That was sending so <u>much love to friend's</u> I can't imagine who it could be but of course I will except all of his love. Who was it please. Well I am very tired so I suppose I had better close and retire. Enclosed find reciept for "Georgian" thanking you again for kindness*
>
> *Your*
M. S. McM
>
> *P.S. Oh, Mr. Bellamy spent yesterday with us.*

I have no idea who Mr. Bellamy is, since this is the first time

---

[13] *The Atlanta Georgian and Evening News,* October 30, 1908, p. 4, at georgiahistoricnewspapers.galileo.usg.edu.

I've seen his name. November 23 was a Monday; Mr. Bellamy had visited on a Sunday, then—a not unusual occurrence among friends. If he happened to have arrived, uninvited, at dinner time (that is to say, near the noon hour), Mattie's mother would simply have set another plate for him and made him feel at home. Perhaps from time to time, this Mr. Bellamy had dropped in at the Wilson farm, where Sophronia, if she had been able, or Betty in her mother's stead, would have added a plate for him.

If this M. S. McMullen is the Mattie McMullen I found in the 1900 census, living in the Jonesboro district but not in the city itself, she is about nineteen years old when she writes. Her handwriting is legible; the message is comprehensible; her style is bright and breezy. We can forgive the errors I have not marked with the pedant's *sic*: incorrectly used apostrophes—*New's, thank's, count's, friend's,* its omission from the word *cant*—writing *except* for *accept*; the misspelling of *receipt*; the lack of punctuation. In the 1900 census, the interview dated June 15 of that year, someone has reported that Mattie, at age eleven, had not been in school at all. Neither had a brother one year older; a fifteen-year-old brother had attended for three months. In the absence of mandatory attendance laws, families decided when their children had acquired enough schooling; Mattie had either attended when she was younger—to what grade level we can't say—or she had been schooled at home.

Mattie's letter does let us know something about Martin. The fact that the purchase was made by money order tells us two things: First, at the time Mattie approached him about taking out the subscription, he had not so much as $4.50 extra cash on his person or within the house. And second, he probably did not have any money in a bank, either, unless it was in a savings account. (If he had a checking account, he would not use it for such a purchase as this.) But, in addition to what the transaction indicates about his relative impecunity, Mattie's delightful letter lets us glimpse a Martin who seems to be quite approachable. He must have liked young people. This one, in particular, takes a jocular and teasing tone with him. Imagine asking him to tell her "Who was it, please?" who had come with talk of "love."

Mattie's letter, unlike those of the other young women whose letters we found, gives no indication of any "love" interest in Martin. (If she did develop a romantic interest in him, she lived near enough to him not to have to resort to letters to signal that interest.) Before getting to the two writing to Martin in the next decade, with talk of love in one instance and of friendship that might have presaged love in the other, I want to share a letter to Martin from his friend, Mack Carnes. Mack's letter takes us back to his and Martin's shared youth; if his correspondent thinks that he is writing about matters of interest to Martin, the letter may contain clues that help to explain why the Martin of the century's second decade appears to be a different person from the Martin of the first.

Chapter Seven
"IN THE NAME OF JESUS, GET SAVED..." MACK CARNES, ASBURY COLLEGE, WILMORE, KENTUCKY, 1908

Mack Carnes arrived at Asbury College in the fall of 1908 and soon became active in student life there—writing to Martin, for instance, about going with other students from Asbury to a convention in Texas, an event that must have occurred soon after his arrival. His letter is dated November 1; he is looking forward to Christmas, though he doesn't yet know whether he will come home for the holiday. The "home" they shared was the Noah's Ark community, but Mack's family lived outside the community's boundaries, in nearby Lovejoy. Mack had long ties to Noah's Ark, however, even when non-resident: land ownership, family connections, a continuous affiliation with the church. When we knew him, Mack was living, at least part-time, in the community—in the family's pre-Civil War plantation house on Carnes Road, where he had been living, apparently full time, in the decades before we knew him. In the year 1930, when he was the census taker for his part of the militia district in which the house sits, he listed his as household number one; in 1940, he and his wife were still living in the same house, household number forty-seven in another census taker's canvass.

Mack Carnes was lay leader of Noah's Ark Methodist church during all the years of our youth, and he held several other leadership roles as well. (As well-brought up young Southerners, we always addressed him, and spoke of him, as "Mister" Mack, as indeed those of our mother's generation continued to do throughout the years. That show of respect, that show of deference, was not a thing one outgrew in the passage into adulthood.) We never knew, however, anything that would have led us to imagine that these two old men, Mr. Mack and our Uncle Martin, ever had been close enough for an exchange of letters. The things that we did know about Mr. Mack were that he was devoted to the church and that he seemed to adore Mrs. Dora Mae, his wife, and our piano teacher. We knew, also, that both continued from their younger days to be a part of the music ministry at Indian Springs Holiness Campground in Flovilla (Butts County), Georgia, where Dora Mae had been a pianist and vocal soloist and Mack continued to play cornet in the orchestra. We did not know anything—maybe because we paid not enough attention—to Mack's connection to Asbury College in Wilmore, Kentucky.

Asbury College, a project entirely conceived by the Reverend John Wesley Hughes, Methodist pastor and evangelist, had been founded in 1890. Hughes intended his college from its beginning to be a "real salvation college"; in its first year, it was known as the Kentucky Holiness College. The Bible was at the center of the curriculum; students began each day with mandatory chapel, and professors started each class with an invocation, which might be given by professor or student. When President Hughes learned (perhaps he was reminded of it—it seems a thing he should have known) that Francis Asbury's 1790 Mt. Bethel Academy, the first such school west of the Alleghenies, had been located just four miles away, he changed his college's name to Asbury and brought a stone from the ruins of the older school to enclose in the cornerstone of the new college's second building. In promoting his school, Hughes touted its accessibility—on the Cincinnati, New Orleans, and Texas Pacific Railroad line, 100 miles from Cincinnati and 240 miles from Chattanooga. (And a long way from Noah's Ark.) Hughes also exclaimed over the beauty of the countryside and must have had its relatively mild climate in mind when he highlighted the region's "healthfulness."

At a distance from populated places, the college was going to have a rural as well as a religious cast. It did not seem to be so rural as to have had an actual farm, worked in part by student labor, as did some colleges begun in Georgia in the same era. (My college—Young Harris, also Methodist—is an example of this, as is Berry College in Rome.) Asbury's curriculum had no agricultural, mechanical, or industrial component at all in the beginning; a business course was added in the second decade. Like other colleges established in other rural settings in the same era, Asbury had a primary and secondary, as well as collegiate division. The town of Wilmore, whose Methodist Church had raised the $1,600 seed money for the new college, had had no school at all before the college broke ground; people were urged to support the new school because it offered educational opportunities, including the lower grade levels, for their children.

Until 1920, enrollment figures did not distinguish between collegiate and pre-collegiate enrollment, and Mack must have been in the pre-collegiate division, for he reports himself in the census record some years later to have completed tenth grade. That, by the way, was much more advanced than it sounds to our ears. Most schools in rural areas went to seventh grade, maybe eighth; and many young people left qualified to teach, if they could pass the tests that were beginning to become standardized in the nineteenth century's last decades. Some schools offered a ninth and tenth grade year, labeling those classes "college preparatory." That tenth-grade completion made Mack a high school graduate, whether there was a diploma awarded or not.

Asbury College began with seven students and one professor; by the end of the year, there were seventy-five students and three professors. By the end of the second year, faculty size grew to eight in number. Within its first decade, Asbury graduated two foreign students—one Persian, one Japanese—each of whom returned to his own country as a missionary. Asbury has always held a reputation for sending out missionaries. One of the most famous—E. (Eli) Stanley Jones—graduated in 1907. One of

Asbury's famous revivals had begun in 1905 in the dorm room of E. Stanley Jones. (These revivals lasted for months.) For a year or so, Jones taught at Asbury, before his call to the mission field—he served in India and became a friend of Gandhi's. He was on staff while Mack was there. Mack mentions some well-known evangelists in his letter to Martin, but he makes no mention of Jones. Who knows, at the time, that he is the company of someone destined for fame?

I am only occasionally going to point out spelling or grammatical errors in Mack's letter. I am too charmed by his spelling of the word *religeon* and by his refusal to let go of the final "e" when forming the participle, as if there were some majesty in the holding on.

> *Asbury College*
>
> *Wilmore, Ky.*
Nov. 1-1908
>
> *Dear Mr. Martin: -*
> *I have come in from dinner, and I thought I would write you a few lines, to keep you from feeling <u>bad</u> and to make you feel good.*
>
> *How are you all getting along? Fine I hope. Guess you are through picking cotton by this time.*
>
> *I am getting on fine. Haveing the best time I ever had in my life I believe.*
>
> *Old Asbury <u>is all</u> that is claimed for it, and more too. Tongue or pen can't begin to tell the real truths that realy (sic) [lie] in the walls of this sacred Institution (sic). I might write all the afternoon about it, and then not tell much, or rather, get into the deep truths as they present themselves only to those who stay here for a season of time. All the students here are not saints by any means. There are some of the worst kind of*

characters, at heart, in school I believe I ever saw. (One boy has been sent home.) But there are so <u>many more</u> godly boys, that the bad boys don't stand any showing at all. They <u>have</u> to obey orders, and it goes hard with them if they don't too.

I don't think the school will be troubled with any more serious cases tho', as those "toughs" that come soon find out that they have to submit or go home, just as they like.

We are now haveing a revival in the College. Bro. Morrison is in Charge (sic). *He is doing some fine and good sound preaching. I wish you was* (sic) *here to take it <u>in</u>. My! my! How he does "skin" the people here. There seems to be a "draw back" or something I don't [know] what, that the meeting is not as good as it ought to [be], but we are praying that God will break all the ice and give us a Pentecostal Revival. And I want it to start with <u>me</u>, too.*

Mack does not further identify the Brother Morrison he has just mentioned, so it is to be assumed Martin recognizes the name, perhaps has heard Morrison preach, either at Indian Springs or at Shingleroof Campground in McDonough, where Martin's mother owned a "tent," or at a convention like the one Mack is soon to describe. The Brother Morrison, whom Mack writes about here, was a Kentucky Methodist, Dr. Henry Clay Morrison, circuit-riding preacher and evangelist, whose favorite arena was the camp meeting. Morrison also published *The Pentecostal Herald* (formerly *The Old Methodist*). In Asbury College's early years, the paper came to its rescue so often, with funds collected through appeals published in the paper, that Morrison was named president in 1910 when Hughes was ousted. Morrison was instrumental in establishing the Asbury Theological Seminary in 1923, and he invited Hughes to return to the school to be the seminary's head. Morrison stepped down from the presidency in 1925 to resume full-time his evangelical career. He returned in 1933; this time his tenure lasted until his death, which occurred while he was preaching a revival in New Jersey in 1940. William Jennings Bryan, famed orator, four times Democratic candidate for president, called Morrison "the greatest pulpit orator on the American continent."[14]

Mack describes Morrison's preaching as "skinning"—probably getting right to the core of the matter and into the hearts of his listeners—but, as of this writing, not so effective as Mack might have expected. He continues with an excited description of a Holiness Convention he had recently attended:

> Say, let me tell you about my trip to the Convention. I had the best time in the world. You ought to have been there. I heard Bro. Bud Robinson preach once. I tell you that man is a sight in this world. I could sit and listen at him a week I do believe and not get tired. I heard some of the best preachers in the Evangelistic field, preach. I tell you the Holiness Movement has got some <u>Giants</u> at work and don't you forget it. There were fourteen of us boys and girls [Asbury was co-ed] went from here and we sure had a time too, going and comeing back. But the [best] time of all times was after we got there and met the Meridian girls and boys. I tell you if those Meridian girls aren't "peaches" I'll give it up. A fellow that would go with one of them a time or two, and didn't fall in love with them, his <u>heart</u> is in a mighty bad condition as sure as you live. I saw Bessie Davis. She is as fine as ever. She received a call to the Mission field while there. And I tell you if her face didn't have a shine of heaven.

Of course, I want to know who this Bessie Davis was, but I cannot find her. She must have been an acquaintance of the two young men, but how they knew her cannot now be discovered, nor can her missionary experience be known. About Brother Bud

---

[14] Matt Kinnel, "Henry Clay Morrison," https://www asbury.edu/academics/resources/library/archives/biographies.

Robinson, however, there is much information available. "Uncle Bud" Robinson, was born Reuben Robinson in Tennessee in 1860, the last of thirteen children in a poor family; the father died in 1872 and in 1876 the mother moved them to Texas, where Reuben (Bud), born with a speech impediment, became one of the "toughs." Completely uneducated, he found what work he could; frequented the beer halls and the dance halls; attended and, we will assume, when he had the money for it, bet on the horse races. At the age of twenty, he was converted during a tent revival; he reported that he threw away the gun he had in one pocket and the deck of cards he had in the other, and that he sought baptism in the local Methodist church. He hesitated to attend Sunday school in the earliest days of his new life—until he was assured by the teacher that he would not be called upon to read.

On the very night of his conversion, however, the illiterate young man with the stutter had heard the call to preach; as soon as he taught himself the rudiments of reading, he received a license to preach and began a course of study at Southwestern University in Georgetown, Texas. Robinson's four years of study there did not reach the level of a college degree, and he never held a pastorate. He joined the Salvation Army while at Southwestern and later found his way into the Church of the Nazarene and onto the board of one of its colleges, all the while preaching at camp meetings all over the country. He claimed to have preached over thirty-two thousand sermons resulting in two hundred thousand conversions, and he authored more than a dozen books. He wrote, as well, a column for the *Herald of Holiness* (that's what he called it; it must have been Morrison's *Holiness Herald*), which Robinson said every Nazarene should be reading, lest he or she fall into serious error.

The fourteen boys and girls from Asbury had probably traveled to Robinson's Texas for a Holiness Convention in Meridian, which had a co-educational college that no longer exists. The conventions were a phenomenon of the Holiness Movement, and they seem to have appealed especially to young people. The

Holiness Movement was at the time of Mack's writing just that—still a "movement" that was only beginning to organize itself into distinct denominations. The Holiness Movement had begun in the early nineteenth century with a strong Methodist imprint. And the churches that grew out of the movement—the Holiness Church, the Pentecostal Church, the Church of the Nazarene, the Free Methodist Church, the Wesleyan Church, and the Salvation Army (the last having originated in England)—all emphasized some belief or practice of John Wesley's, particularly the doctrine of sanctification or "going on to perfection," which was what the "holiness" movement sought.

Noah's Ark Methodist Church may be said to have had a Holiness aspect well past the mid-twentieth century, no matter the leanings of the young seminarians from Emory University who were sent by the bishop to fill its pulpit one Sunday each month. We did hear sermons on sanctification, which I have not heard preached on much since my childhood. Our services—whether the monthly preaching service or the Sunday school assembly, even our revivals—lacked the fervor of a real Holiness service, but there was time for testimonials and extemporaneous prayer that held opportunity for the movement of the Holy Spirit. When the church withdrew from the North Georgia Conference of the Methodist Church, there were questions of polity and governance, not doctrinal or worship style differences, that led to the separation.

With his admiration for the evangelistic preachers and his desire that the Pentecostal revival begin with him, the young Mack felt no hesitancy in extending his personal witness into Martin's life, especially since Martin seems before this time not to have made a public declaration of faith.

> *I tell you Martin, if you want to be free and be free indeed, and go around in this world and have a good time, you will have to get religeon. Religeon is the only thing that has given me any peace. Glory to Jesus. He has been sweeter to me since I came here than ever before I thank God I'm here.*

Now Martin, I am your friend. I love you truly, and <u>now</u> it is time you must give your heart to God. You need God in your heart and life. You will soon be passed the "deadline." You have lived with out (sic) salvation long enough. You remember when you was (sic) sick last winter; how near you came going out of this world into the <u>great beyond</u> without God and with out hope. How you realized your need of a Saviour (sic), don't you? I tell you, you will never know how my heart was burdened for you, as I thought of your condition. And I verily believe that it was the prayers of some good people at <u>Old Noah's Ark</u>, that reached God and brought about your recovery. Now Martin, listen just a moment. No doubt you said in your heart, when you was (sic) sick, that if God would let your get up again you would do better and get religeon or (relief). Now didn't you? Now through God's mercies he has spared your life and given you a chance. And,—it will soon be a year. And,—if you go on and reject the blood of Christ and refuse to let him in, you may get sick again about the same time,—and,—you may seek God's face and call up on (sic) His name, and,—He may not hear your cries. <u>Such</u> [a] thing does happen sometimes. But I hope it wont (sic) be that way with you. In the name of Jesus, get saved son and lets (sic) go to heaven together and shout and praise God forever and ever. Amen. Hallelujah! What say you. I hope you will. Bless God.

Apparently, Uncle Charlie had thought about going to Asbury too. Mack and Charlie were the same age—twenty years old in the year Mack is writing. When Mack makes the inquiry about Charlie but says that he will wait until he has some free time to write to him, there is all the evidence we need to signal to us that Mack carried a burden on his heart for Martin's salvation. Even if his theological understanding seems youthfully shallow, that burden is so heavy that Mack would make time, right then and there, while he was thinking about Martin, to write to him; a letter to Charlie could await another day.

Excerpt of Letter from Mack A. Carnes, 1908

Say, is Charlie getting ready to come up here after Christmas. Tell him I said to take new courage and press the battle and come on. His place is waiting for him. I don't know whether I will get to come [home?] Christmas or not. I wont (sic) know until I get ready to start. But he can Come (sic) on just the same.

I will try to write to him sometime soon. I don't know when though. I have so much to do I don't have much time to write.

Will have to close and get ready for Church tonight.
With love to all. Be a good boy and get <u>saved</u>.

Good Bye,
Your True Friend
Mack Carnes.

It does seem that Martin's life changed after his brush with death. The change may not have been apparent to Mack Carnes a year later. There might not have been a dramatic conversion experience such as Martin's friend seemed to wish for him—a "real salvation" event, with a public confession of faith. Whatever change there was—in character, in personality, in faith—might have had a more slowly evolving, less dramatic nature. Martin did become active enough in his home church toward the end of the next decade, about the time of the last of the letters we're examining, to develop a close friendship with the pastor whom his family invited to return to deliver his eulogy thirty-five years later.

In the last of the letters, those from Sister in 1915 and 1916 and those from Mag in 1917, Martin seems to be a nicer—can we say, a better—person than he had been in the earlier decade. He has become a "man of good will." To Mag, who wrote those words, he is a kind man, solicitous of other people's feelings. Though Mag is the last of the young women from whom the letters came, I will turn to her before coming at last to Sister.

Chapter Eight
"It will be to me as if all the rays of sunshine shut out of my life." Mag, Homer, Demorest, Fowlstown, 1917

There is between 1908 and 1915 a seven-year gap in the letters. Martin lost his mother in those years. Two brothers married and started their families. We don't know whether Charlie went to Asbury to study; we do know that he married toward the end of those seven years, or soon thereafter. Perhaps Mack had not considered that Martin might have wanted to go to Asbury too. Apparently, Martin had never spoken about doing such a thing; had he done so, Mack would have written about Martin as well as about Charlie in connection with the school.

If Mack, at twenty, seems a little old to be starting what is in effect a high school program, then Martin at thirty would seem more unlikely still to be taking that step. Martin also, as far as we can tell from the records, lacked sufficient preparation for enrollment in a college program. We find, for example, in his self-reporting for the census, that his formal schooling had ended with fourth grade. It should be noted, however, that S. S. (Sophronia Susan or, maybe, Susan Sophronia) Turner, who will become Martin's mother, reported herself to be a teacher in the US Census of 1870. Perhaps she did most of the "schooling" that her children received below the high school level. In an era when credentialing, except for the professions, was not yet of much importance, reporting only a few years in school was not unusual. The oldest son in the Wilson family, John, did attend high school—at a time when there were very few high schools; questions about why the younger children received less formal schooling can probably not be answered these many decades later.

There were colleges in Georgia to which Martin might have gained admission—if he had sought it—at some level below the collegiate. But probably he did not seek it. Beyond the question of age was the fact that he had an occupation, one, moreover, that did not require any more schooling than he already had. He was a farmer who had learned husbandry in the apprenticeship of a family farm. Any learning beyond that was enrichment, and enrichment might be attained through any number of avenues: attending church and various other meetings (the conventions his correspondents wrote about), reading, conversing and conversing's companion pieces—debating, politicking, and storytelling. Even the farming might be studied through reading magazines and journals and attending demonstrations and lectures, all readily enough available, at least in the county-seat towns or at regional centers.[15]

With his farming life Martin seems to have been content. There are neither measures of success in the enterprise left in the record (beyond his farm's survival through the Great Depression) nor descriptions of satisfaction in the work, but almost all his correspondents do mention farming in their letters. Mack asks, for instance, whether he has completed the cotton picking, and Mag, whose letters form the focus for this chapter, assuming the topic will interest him, writes to him about the potato harvest on the south Georgia farm where she is boarding with a farm family.

Mag, whose hometown is Homer, Georgia (county seat of Banks County), writes also about a county fair in a town she

---

[15] See, for example, George Frederick Hunnicutt, ed. *Southern Crops as Grown and Described by Successful Farmers and Published from Time to Time in the Southern Cultivator*. ([Atlanta, GA.]: The Cultivator Publishing Company, 1908). Available at books.google.com. Search by title. The articles in *Southern Crops* came from teachers at agricultural colleges as well as from farmers themselves, but those from individual farmers were greater in number.

designates "D." She also mentions the Southeastern Fair, new when she writes about it and soon to become a great attraction for farm families. The Southeastern Fair was not far from Martin's home; it was located in the Lakewood section of Atlanta, relatively near the Clayton County line. At the Southeastern Fair, and at the county fairs, too, there were shows of fine cattle, dairy cows, sheep, goats, and all other manner of animal; crop yield reports and samples; and displays of award-winning craft of all kinds—from sewing and quilting to flower arranging and baking and canned good displays—all brought to the fair in hopes the entrant would win a ribbon to signal proud achievement.

I think the "D" that Mag mentions denotes the town of Demorest. Demorest is in Habersham County, just north of Mag's home county of Banks. The town is the site of a college, one that Mag may have attended as part of her teacher training. The college's founding dates to the same era as Asbury's; its name—Piedmont College—was chosen to reflect its location, the piedmont region at the southern end of the Appalachians. The college had begun as J. S. Green Collegiate Institute in 1897; it was established by Demorest Home, Mining, and Improvement Company to provide education from the first grade through the junior year in college. Though its first president was a Methodist clergyman (who had been president of Young Harris College), Piedmont College would come to have a long association with the Congregational Church, which took over its operation in 1901, when Green Collegiate Institute fell into financial difficulties. It was the new Congregational leadership that changed the name of the school.

The connection to Methodism remained strong, however. There is today in the town of Demorest, situated on the college grounds or right adjacent to them, a Federated Church—both United Methodist and Congregational, the only such partnership I know anything about in the whole state. Throughout its history, Demorest Methodist Church had been on a charge with other churches, usually the church in Clarksville whose pastor was assigned one Sunday in the month to the Demorest church. When the Clarksville church decided in 1947 to ask for a full-time appointment, "other plans had to be made for Demorest," the historian of Demorest Methodist Church wrote in a report sent to the conference in 1951. The report continues:

> After much planning and careful consideration it was decided to Federate (sic) with the Union Congregational Church which also had a small membership. With the two groups pooling their resources and working together it was thought that a more far-reaching program for both churches could be carried on. A plan was worked out by which the Congregationalists pay one-third, the Methodists one-third, and Piedmont College one-third of the pastor's salary. The pastor serves as College chaplain and teaches one course in religion at the College. Each church retains it denominational connections and Methodists are as much Methodist now as ever. Services are held in the Congregational church. Each church keeps a separate roll and the women's societies meet separately except for special courses which are planned jointly, but both groups compose the membership of the Federated Church.[16]

* * *

It would have been easy to surmise, if we had not already dismissed the idea, that Martin met both Sister and Mag at Piedmont College. The question of how he came to be a friend to these women begs for an answer. The easiest explanation would be that

---

[16] N. Evie Gillespie, "History of Demorest Methodist Church [1951]." Unpublished paper at https://s3-us-west-2.amazonaws.com/pittsarchives/mss028/pdf/Demorest.pdf. Accessed June 12, 2020.

someone in his family had friendship or kinship ties with the girls' families. There is some evidence of that in one of Sister's letters when she asks about the McMullen family in Jonesboro. Another possibility—how likely a possibility we can't say—would be that Martin had forsaken farming in the early or mid-1910s and found other work, maybe on a railroad, as he was supposed to have done early in the century's first decade, and that the work took him into their area. The letters give no hint of that, either.

Mag, whose surname I cannot find, had family in Demorest. The Demorest kin can be found, because, in the only instance since M. S. McMullen wrote almost ten years earlier, we have a family name, even if, this time, it's not the letter writer's own. In the second letter of the two we have from her, Mag offers condolences to Martin in the recent loss of an aunt and says that her cousin and childhood friend, Julia Gillespie, has died. The Gillespie family consisted in 1910 of the widowed father E. A. Gillespie, a farmer; three daughters, Myrt, Evie, and Julia; and one son, Marvin. The daughters are twenty-two, nineteen, and seventeen years old; the son is thirteen. Mag is especially worried about Evie's bereavement when Julia dies. This suggests that Evie was still unmarried at the time and that the oldest sister probably now had her own family. That turns out not to be the case, however, for Myrt is found in the 1920 census still at home, at the age of thirty-two. (It is Evie, who also remained unmarried, who wrote the history of Demorest Methodist Church.)

We have no clear reason to assume that Martin knew the Gillespies. When she writes about Julia's death, Mag spells out for him the particulars of her closeness to Julia. However, there is something in the way she writes of Evie as a survivor, mentioning only her, that makes it appear that Martin might have known those two sisters, at least casually, at the same time he knew their cousin Mag. If we can convince ourselves that he knew them, then we can convince ourselves that he had spent some time in Demorest in some capacity other than as a guest of Mag's at a county fair.

The first of the Mag letters is dated May 10, 1917. If Mag is near in age to Julia Gillespie, she is about twenty-four; Martin is thirty-nine. Mag's letter is a love letter—or at least a letter that professes her love, which she realizes is not quite returned to her. The letters he has written since they were last together have been "chilly": she is afraid that he will sense a deep despondency in reading the one she is now writing, and, at the end of the letter, she asks him to burn all her letters. Enclosed in the letter is a brief newspaper announcement of an upcoming marriage:

> BALDWIN-WILSON
> Mr. and Mrs. C. S. Baldwin, of Madison, announce the engagement of their daughter, Genie Maude, to Mr. Jacob Martin Wilson, the wedding to take place in June. No cards.

She does not give the name of the paper in which she found the notice. She probably knows Martin's full name and knows that he is not the groom-to-be. Nevertheless, she begins the letter with a question about the wedding announcement.

> *Homer, Ga.*
> *May 10, 1917*
>
> Dear Martin,
>   *Does this mean you? I can't quite believe it and yet there is a possibility of it being you. But if it be you, why did you not tell me about it before it came to my eyes through the paper? Well, heres (sic) wishing you all the wishes for your future happiness.*
>   *Is this why your letters have been so <u>chilly</u>? You have not seemed like yourself since I came from there. Oh, Martin, I miss you dreadfully! I thought for a long time I would not ask why you felt just as you do and then I know too, that your devotions and attentions have been altogether for the purpose of <u>giving pleasure</u> instead of <u>receiving it</u>, which shows a good will. This has been received by me with all the gratitude and*

appreciation that is possible. Now, dear Heart, I'm sure that my heart has not betrayed nor deceived me and that it is full of pure love for you. I have made myself appear quite foolish and silly to have been so bold and tell you of it, but you are the only man I have talked to so freely. I have been so sad and lonely since I came away and can not (sic) see you any more.

Since she "came away," since she "came from there"? The letter is addressed to Martin in Jonesboro. Where did she stay if she visited him in Jonesboro? Of course, he lived with his sister, so it is possible that she visited with them, Betty serving as hostess and chaperone, and that no one would have looked askance at such goings-on. That's possible, but it is highly unlikely. There was extended family—she could have stayed with Wiley and Nola, with Turner and Jessie, with one of the family's aunts (maybe the Aunt Sallie whom she mentions in her last letter). Perhaps she, like Sister, had a connection to the McMullen family and visited him while staying with that family. When was the visit? The letter is dated May; they have been writing to each other since the visit. I think it very likely that she had visited during the Christmas season. That would make it, indeed, a long time since they had seen each other.

If there has been a five-month separation, then it is easy enough to see that she has missed him "dreadfully" and that she is "sad and lonely." It is hardly possible for readers a century later, however, living in a time of casual sexual encounters and experimentation, to read words of "giving" and "receiving" pleasure with the realization that their meaning was most likely limited to social intercourse—to the arts of conversation and letter writing. But I maintain that that is exactly what she means, though I will allow them some handholding and kissing, and, perhaps, a little heavier petting. She may have been "foolish" and "silly" and "bold," but only in having told him how she felt. And she wants her confession of love not to be burdensome to him. He should not write out of a sense of obligation she tells him next—that would be a "sacrifice" she does not want him to take upon himself.

> *You have no idea* [the letter continues] *what a suffering it is to me, but I knew it would come. I realize more fully than ever that you do not and can not* (sic) *love me in return and that I mean very little to you. Knowing this, I can see how very, very, good to me you have been and what a task and an unpleasant job it must be to you to try to write to me, and I'm going to ask you not to write any more unless you really wish to and can derive a bit of pleasure from it. You don't know how hard it is for me to tell you this and when your letters stop and I can not* (sic) *hear from you anymore it will be to me as* [if] *all the rays of sunshine shut out of my life. I'm not so selfish and narrow minded as to expect or even want you to commit yourself to any task or sacrifice except as you really wish.*

Oh, I am so upset for her—and with her! How can she paint herself so meek, how can she feel herself so unworthy? I know we can't fault her writing style. What she is trying to express is difficult to put into words. She is probably writing just as she speaks, and we can't imagine what words would have followed any one of these declarations if she had been face to face with him in conversation. But it is likely that there have been conversations in the past in this vein. She indicates that to be the fact: There is something unsaid, perhaps too painful for her to write and too painful, she fears, for him to read, that makes her sure that, though he is a friend, the friendship does not, cannot, will not, reach the level of a committed love.

She continues as if it has occurred to her how pathetic she must seem. She acknowledges that he is likely to read this outpouring as an example of her moodiness, and she expressly tells him that nothing he has done (or failed to do) is to blame for her despondency:

> *Now, you think no doubt that this is another spell of blues I'm possessed of and that perhaps I am disappointed in some little thing you unknowingly have failed to do. Don't think*

this, I'm not the least angry and have not been and you will always be the same dear, sweet man to me and my love still lives for you as ever. Oh, can I make you understand the situation right. I wish I could. It is that you have been sacrificing enough for me and that I just must not expect you to continue. I think of you a thousand times a day and my poor little Bluebirds (sic) message will always bear the same wishes and love to you. Now, try to remember me as a pure innocent and would be Christian, whose love for you will never fade.

Good by
Mag
Please burn all my letters.

"Letters." There were more, then, just as we thought. He probably didn't burn them, though all except this and one other became lost over time. And he didn't discontinue his letter-writing, either. But the tone of the letters that follow this one must have been different. His last letter, to which she sends the following reply, has evidently reached Mag in Fowlstown, Georgia. It appears that she has taken a teaching position; there is mention of the Halloween program at the schoolhouse. And she is boarding with a farming family named Owens. Now she adds the information about the potato crop.

In this letter, Mag's tone has certainly changed, whether in response to a change in his letters, in exhaustion at the psychic toll this relationship has placed on her, or in resignation at what the fates have in store for them. She mentions nothing of love, or of burdening him with the "sacrifice" of attuning himself to her needs. The letter almost lacks any emotive content at all, beyond one evocative memory and one prospective wish. The memory is about attending the fair with Martin, probably in Demorest and probably in a year earlier than this one. "Many things happened that day . . . which I'll never forget." The wish aligns with their religious understandings. They seem to be committed Christians who have discussed their faith with each other. She describes hers as a growing faith and trusts that the two will know each other in their "home above." Writing in this vein seems natural in a letter that has in part been intended as a condolence note. It makes a fitting farewell, too, a final break, to their friendship on this earth.

Fowlstown, Ga
Oct. 27, 1917

Dear Martin,

You are not expecting a letter from me now, I know, but I am up this beautiful, clear, bright morning with my mind full of thoughts of you and other friends who are in sorrow. Your letter bearing the news of the death of your Aunt Sallie came to me and I wish to express my heartfelt sympathy in the loss of one whom (sic) *I knew meant so much to you.*

The same day your letter came, I received another telling me of the death of Julia Gillespie, my cousin and constant companion of childhood school-days. This was sad news to me and I feel so sorry for Evie who will miss her sister so much.

Martin, I wonder if you would be glad to know that I am trying harder and really think I am a better girl and stronger christian (sic) *than when you knew me. I think my sins have been more of omission than commission. I trust that when our lives shall have been ended here that you and I will have a home above and know each other there.*

How about the cold up there? We have had a killing frost here so potato digs are the order of the day. Mr. Owens says he made seventy-five bu. of potatoes on one fourth of an acre. Isn't that a good yield?

Excerpt of Letter from Mag, 1917, with its "Kind Wishes"

Pretty soon sugar boiling and purliens [praleins?] will be in full blast. You know that is new to me and I am anxious for it to come off.

Did I tell you of our Halloween social at the school-house? It would take too long to tell you all but enough to say it was a success.

Glad you went to the S. E. Fair. I know it must have been great. The fair at D. was very good. Many things happened that day we went, of which I'll never forget.

Yesterday night I went up to Bainbridge with a bunch of friends to see Mutt and Jeff divorced. It was an evening of great fun. I thought Mutt and Jeff were good but I did not care for the chorus part (girls part) of it.

I have much to do to-day so I'll say good by and get busy. Kind wishes.

Yours, Mag

"Kind wishes." There we leave off speculations about Mag and turn our attention at last to Sister, beginning with even more far-reaching speculations. During the time that Mag was writing to Martin, Sister was no longer writing, as far as we know. We have only three letters from Sister; one dated and two undated; the dated one is from June 1915; to one other I've assigned also a 1915 date. The last was probably composed a year later, in the fall of 1916. Mag's letters are both from 1917. I think, with no evidence whatsoever to back up the conjecture, that the two young women had known each other; that something had come between Sister and Martin, and that Mag had tried to fill a void that she came to realize she could not fill.

Chapter Nine
"I THINK YOU ARE THE MOST THOUGHTFUL BOY . . ." SISTER, MAYSVILLE AND LULA, 1915 AND 1916

On a cold day in the fall, while northwest Georgia was under flood warning from recent—and continuing—rain, I drove away from my home in northeast Georgia under overcast skies—and occasional rain—in search of Sister. My first stop was at the old courthouse in downtown Jefferson, then in the final stages of restoration, where the Jackson County Historical Society maintains an impressive collection of primary sources and secondary accounts. The women working there wanted to be helpful, but what do you do with a researcher who doesn't even know a name? I did know Sister's hometown—Maysville—and that might be a start. They brought me the Tax Digest for Maysville in 1915 and I looked through the record for the two militia districts that encompassed the area.

In one of Sister's letters, she named an Irene residing at her Maysville home. I assume that this Irene was her sister, but I have no way of knowing what the relationship was. The name was, however, the only name we had for anyone residing in Sister's home. Perhaps I could find an Irene in the records. If she owned some personal property, she might have paid some tax on it. There was a "Lunie I. Wheeler," who owned an automobile and a horse and buggy on which she paid taxes. Could I make that middle initial stand for "Irene"? Could I make "Lunie" read "Lenna"—surely the handwritten entry in the Tax Digest allowed for that. I found a Lenna Wheeler in the census record for that district, with a baby sister, Katie, who was eleven years old in 1900. A baby sister, as well as an older one, might endearingly be called "Sister." The Wheeler family seemed to be a promising lead; if that baby Katie became our Sister, she is twenty-six years old when she writes to our thirty-seven-year-old uncle in 1915.

The Jackson County Historical Society had a nice folder with accounts of the Maysville's early history, but Sister writes as if she lives some distance from the town: "I will want you to arrive at Maysville and [then] home about July 30," Sister writes to Martin. She has already informed him that they don't usually have ice at home because it is too far to go into town for it. Most towns had ice plants in those days, and most homes owned "ice boxes" in which to preserve the ice they brought home in blocks. In both Maysville and Ashland, from where she posts a letter while visiting a sister (alas, unnamed), Sister is so far out in the country that she must write with a pencil, and she apologizes for having neither pen nor ink. If her Maysville home was out in the country, it could have been in either Jackson County or Banks; the town lies in both. If she is a member of the Wheeler family, the home was in Jackson.

From Jefferson, I drove to Demorest, some thirty or so miles north, to Piedmont College. I was searching for Mag, too, as well as for Sister, since Mag had mentioned Demorest (or at least a "D" town that seems to have been Demorest) in a letter. It seemed logical to me that the two young women had attended college together as part of their teacher preparation, and what better place—so near to their hometowns—than Piedmont? Piedmont's archivist showed me 1913 and 1914 editions of *The Mountain Lantern*, a precursor to the college's yearbook, and we examined the only records of early enrollment that are available. The records appear to have been reconstructed from names of alumni who stayed in touch with the college or who made contact decades later; the class lists are so incomplete as to be useless. Of course, the lists would be of no use to a researcher who knew no surname in any case. If Martin Wilson, seemingly too old for college, had gone there and met two young women who became his correspondents, he left no record.

We did find Marvin Gillespie—Evie and Julia's brother, and Mag's cousin—in the *Lantern*, in his sixteenth and seventeenth years, playing on the basketball team. (There are photos of the teams in both years.) A child of the town, it is logical to assume that he followed his sisters, Myrt, Evie, and Julia, onto the Piedmont campus. We did not find his sisters, however, in any record in the archivist's office. I did later find Evie in the report of the American Missionary Society, Congregational Church, available online, teaching in Piedmont's elementary school division in 1917. She lived in Demorest all her life, filling an active role as educational, civic, and cultural leader. Her brother, Marvin, became the postmaster. "Oh, Gillespie," the archivist said. "That is a well-known name here."

On the drive back to Jackson County, I detoured through Homer and passed a road that would have taken me to Lula. I thought about Mag, whose home was in Homer, and about Sister, whose last letter comes from Lula. How relatively close these places are to one another—Maysville, Homer, Lula, Demorest. Even Ashland, in Franklin County, is not so far away, Banks County (Maysville, Homer, Lula) having been carved out of Franklin. But how far away all of them are from Jonesboro, Stockbridge, and Noah's Ark.

We know Martin was planning to visit Maysville and that he was in Demorest at least once. To get to these places Martin would have taken the train. He would have boarded in Jonesboro, probably, or maybe Flippen, and traveled to Atlanta. In Atlanta, he would have purchased a ticket to Athens. (It is possible, of course, that he secured a direct ticket to Athens; I didn't examine all the rail line possibilities.) From Athens, he could reach Maysville by way of the Northeastern Railroad on the line it had constructed in the 1870s between Athens and Lula, with Maysville the fourth stop north of Athens.

The final northern terminus in the state legislature's incorporation plan for the railroad was to be Clayton, near the North Carolina line, just a few miles north of Tallulah Falls, with its tourist-attracting waterfalls and magnificent gorge. It was not the tourist industry that prompted the railroad building, however. The tourist industry grew in importance only in the next few decades, a development no doubt facilitated in part because the rail lines were in place. The initial railway construction was envisioned as a boon to Georgia's industrial growth since it would supply access to the mineral riches of the east Tennessee region around Knoxville, to the north and west of Clayton.

Construction on the Northeastern Railroad began south of Clayton—in Lula, a settlement whose name honors the daughter of a major shareholder in the Northeastern. (The Northeastern never did reach Clayton; the line that did run through Clayton was the Tallulah Falls Railroad, with its final terminus in Franklin, North Carolina, which it reached only in 1907.) In May 1876, a news account reported the Northeastern line to be "running from Lula to Harmony Grove. Track laying toward Athens [was] progressing."[17]

Trains still come into Lula on two different standard gauge tracks (nine pass through each day), and the town celebrates an annual "Railroad Days" festival. The festival is a nostalgic look back to the town's prosperous era. The festival was established some forty years ago—with that date itself being forty years later than the town's heyday—in the manner of small towns everywhere celebrating the past and attempting to generate interest and income. An announcement in 2018 promises renewed prosperity. Lula will be an inland terminus, an inland port of sorts, its city boosters claim, because of its rail link with the port of Savannah, though the railhead will be located outside the town itself in an industrial park more closely associated with nearby Gainesville than with Lula.[18]

When the Northeastern Railroad became fully operational between Athens and Lula, it had depots at Center, Nicholson,

---

[17] *The Forest News, May 1876.* Excerpt in *Jackson County Historical Society News*, Vol. 15, No. 4, July 2008. Also, in "Railroads," in Angela Gary and Jana Adams. *Our Land and Time. A History of Jackson County, Georgia.* Mike Buffington, ed., (Jefferson, GA. Mainstreet Newspapers, 2000, [section] 3. [page] 1.

[18] The city reported from the *Gainesville Times* (December 8, 2018): "Governor announces new inland terminal location in northeast Hall County on Highway 365—Lula to feel impact." At cityoflula.com

Harmony Grove, Maysville, Gillsville, and Lula. Center was only seven miles from downtown Athens; the next stop was at someone's farm before there was the Nicholson name to designate the area. (The town gets its name from the rail line's president.) Harmony Grove is today's Commerce; today, it is much larger than Maysville, but at the end of the nineteenth and the beginning of the twentieth century, the towns were rivals. North of Maysville were the stops at Gillsville, a pottery center—then and now—and Lula.

When Maysville was incorporated in 1879, its limits were "three fourths of a mile in every direction from the Northeastern Railroad depot." Most towns that date from the late nineteenth-century railroad-building era have city boundaries set in exactly this fashion. Maysville's railroad depot no longer exists; often in small towns, even after the tracks were taken up, depots were left standing. These days they are likely to be officially designated historical landmarks, and they are finding other uses—as business offices, perhaps, or more frequently, as tourist offices or community centers.

Maysville, before its incorporation, was informally known as "the Brick Store," for the business that was, before the coming of the railroad, about the only enterprise in the area. It was housed in a brick structure, apparently the only such commercial building north of Athens. The Maysville name probably harkens back to a landowner from the 1840s, though some accounts, including the town's own web page, link it to a rail line official. In its heyday, the town supported a chair factory (there is a caner in business today) and a shoe and leather goods factory, too. There were also dry goods or general merchandise stores; a milliner; four physicians; a four-bed hospital; two veterinarians; two lawyers; a cottonseed oil press; a fertilizer plant; two telephone exchanges—one in the depot, the other in one of the general merchandise stores; and, in the decade after the Sister story, even a movie theater. There was a livery stable, a garage, and a bicycle repair shop. When cotton was the principal crop, as many as eighteen thousand bales of cotton were shipped out on the rail line.

The town is bisected by its single railroad track. The Northeastern Railroad Company, which laid the track, was consolidated into the Southern Railway in 1899; today the line is Norfolk Southern. Some Maysville businesses hugged the hill above the track, their front doors and their raised sidewalk facing the track. A few faced a side road that crossed the railroad track before winding its way uphill past the road that ran in front of the other shops and perpendicular to it. That side road serves, more or less, as the boundary between Jackson and Banks Counties at that point. A vote early in the twentieth century let the city decide whether it wanted to be annexed into one county's jurisdiction, leaving the other's jurisdiction a thing of the past. The vote was for Banks County, but there was a court case, upheld on appeal, which set the vote aside, and, apparently, during the century following that vote, not another one has been attempted.

There were businesses located below the track, also, on the side opposite the highway (today's State Route 98) that parallels the track. Most buildings today, in both locations, are empty, the businesses long since departed. Between the track and the street serving the businesses on the hill lies an open space, a sort of town green, used today as site of an annual Autumn Leaf Festival. This festival was begun by people who wanted the town, for a weekend at least, no longer to look like a ghost town. Today, the town touts a healthy population growth, and city planners eagerly await new businesses that they hope to bring into town to occupy the old buildings.

The first of Sister's letters is the one that bemoans the pencil writing and the lack of ice to make iced tea. If the two little complaints might seem to be marks of a relative poverty, there are other indications that the family is well-off—perhaps situated so nicely that an older sister could have owned an automobile as well as a horse and buggy. Sister's home, for instance, though it seems to be way out in the country, does have a telephone. It is also easy to imagine from the letter she writes from the Ashland sister's house, from which she probably made the telephone call, that the sister has married into a family of substance and standing.

Uncle Martin's Sister

This letter has a date—June 25, 1915. That was a Friday; it was an unseasonably cold day; she will be guest of honor at a Saturday evening soirée. It is unclear whether that event will be hosted by her sister or by a neighbor; perhaps it was a church or community event, one that gave special recognition to visitors. Sister is going to play tennis on the Friday afternoon, and she wishes Martin were there to play a set with her. The main point of the letter seems to be to confirm an invitation for Martin to visit, with assurances that everyone will welcome him, and to detail such travel plans as his arrival time, a little more than a month in the future.

Ashland, Ga
June 25, 1915

Dear Mr. Martin,

See, I'm visiting now. Am having a great time. Will be here till Sun. I will be guest of honor at a social entertainment Sat night.

Going to play tennis this afternoon, but the game will not be complete without you. [First part written in ink; now she switches to pencil.] *I will have to use a pencil and I do despise to write with a pencil. I'm ashamed to send you such writing as this. It is cloudy and cold here. I have on my coat too believe me.* [On a June 25th!]

The folks here and at home talk as big about when Mr. Martin and friends come as I. They say I will have to bring you to Ashland a day or so and guess they will have to Boss. You don't understand about Boss but you will find out later. There's not much to it.

It is early enough in the friendship for her salutation to be "Mr. Martin." Or perhaps, she uses that form in acknowledgment of a difference in their ages. He has apparently visited before, though at that time, or at those times, it seems that he was one member of a larger party of visitors. This may be the first visit he plans to make as the sole invited guest; though she mentions Mr. Martin *and friends*, the letter reads as if it is only Martin who will visit this time. Sister also sends farming news to this farmer friend of hers. It is a single sentence, but perhaps she thinks it will open visions to play out in his mind.

> *There were twenty-five here at sister's yesterday for dinner* [she writes], *part were thrasher hands.*

I don't know what the Ashland farmers were threshing—wheat, perhaps, or rye. One hundred years later, the state is the country's leading producer of rye. What I see in the northeastern corner of Georgia where I live—a short drive away from Sister's Maysville—is hay baling, not threshing. One hay baler makes relatively quick work, several times a year, of the hay baling on the farm facing my subdivision's entry onto Boone Road in rural Jackson County. The man operating the baler is probably the farm's owner, and the harvesting no longer is an occasion for noontime feasting.

Though my childhood home was in Uncle Martin's farming community, I must consult books, read a newspaper's retrospective or its occasional human-interest story, or visit a farm's living history museum to find a picture of a thrashing (threshing) day. The historical farm, especially if it's in Nebraska, is more easily visited virtually than in person. A Nebraska farm story surely differs from a Georgia story in its particulars, but a threshing day is still a threshing day, and the story of a huge communal meal is strikingly the same as in rural Georgia. In York, Nebraska, the day began early. The vignettes included here come from an oral history compiled for the Wessel farm museum's online site. The stories retain the speaking style of the men and women being interviewed.

A big huge threshing machine . . . it was a big old steam engine that run it. The man that run that, if he happened to be threshing at your place, he'd come before breakfast and he would fire up that steam engine so he'd get enough steam so he could run that day. And then you had to, the ladies had to feed him and the man that ran the separator breakfast. And then of course, they had to feed all them hungry men at noon, and there would be, well, there'd be twelve running the racks and there would be some hauling the grain away . . . and the poor ladies, they had hard work to feed all those.[19]

Another account in the same source mentions lunch at ten, then at noon, and then, again, at four—supplemented by sandwiches and snacks. *These folks feed a person here,* Sister exclaimed. Reporters for the Nebraska farm's account remembered decades later the chores assigned to them as children: the little girl watching in the early morning for the arrival of the threshers so she could put out the bench and the pails of soapy water for the workers to wash up before dinner; the young boys carrying cold water from the well to the field, one mentioning even the burlap wrapped around the jugs to keep the water cool; the little boy, now a grown man and probably an old one at that, seeming still to be drooling over the caramel and the chocolate pies spread out on the dessert table.

The food was the fondest memory—from the women killing the chickens in the early morning (the report calls it a "slaughter") to the piles of fried chicken sitting on the serving table. One reporter said that sometimes there was "a contest from all the women putting up a big meal at noon [but, he added] they worked together too." Another said, "Older girls worked in the

---

[19] Claudia Reinhardt, "Harvesting Wheat." Wessels Living History Farm. https://livinghistoryfarm.org/farmingin the 20s/intro/machine/harvesting-wheat/. Accessed May 24, 2020.

kitchen, helping cook platters of fried chicken, potatoes and gravy, beans and squash, homemade bread and butter, pies and cake and much more."[20]

From Georgia—this time we are in the mountains, some sixty, sixty-five road miles north and west of Maysville, across Neel's Gap and at the foot of Blood Mountain—comes an account that contrasts harvesting before the advent of farm machinery to harvesting afterward. Ethelene Dyer Jones describes the difference in her grandfather's farming community after he bought a threshing machine. She begins with her family's farm in Choestoe, Union County, Georgia, by describing the hand labor in the flailing process that separated grain pod from stalk. With so much done by hand, only small acreage was given over to the growing of grains.

> If our crop was small, not much planted in either wheat or rye, we did threshing in the old-fashioned way, flailing the grain.
>
> This was accomplished by spreading a canvas sheet on the ground and placing grain on it. Then, with another sheet over the grain, we took sticks and beat out the seeds, a process we called flailing. Before we put another supply of grain on the sheet to be flailed, the grain we had beaten out had to be separated from the straw and scooped up into containers for winnowing later. This process of beating a small amount at the time went on until our whole crop of wheat or rye was separated from the seed pods.[21]

After describing the winnowing (which required a light breeze and more hand labor that the writer plainly labels *tedious*), she highlights the changes the use of farm machinery brought to her community:

---

[20] Ibid.
[21] Etheleen Dyer Jones. "On the Farm. Threshing Times." *The Union Sentinel*, Blairsville, Ga. July 24, 2011. At rootsweb.com>~gaunion. Accessed May 26, 2020.

Then the threshing machine came . . . and farmers grew larger fields of grain because the process of getting the grain from the pods was less time-consuming. My grandfather [Francis Joseph Collins, farmer and State Representative, she has elsewhere identified him] . . . purchased the [first] machine. . . . [I]n my childhood, I can remember "the threshers" coming. At first, I have been told, and an old faded photograph shows this, Grandpa pulled his threshing machine with a steer team, and somehow had it hooked up so that the animals provided the power to operate the machine, with the necessary pulleys and belts.

Later he purchased a gasoline-powered tractor with huge steel wheels. This became the means of his pulling the threshing machine from farm to farm and also provided the power necessary to operate the thresher. The threshing team made stops at the farms on the circuit that had grain to be threshed. It was a sort of carnival day at our farm when all the threshing gear and the workers arrived. My mother and the neighborhood women—for they helped each other—depending on which farm was on schedule for the day's work—fed the workers a great spread of food at the noon meal which we called dinner then.[22]

The straw, sweet smelling but unfit for animal fodder, that was left over from the flailing was collected to be stuffed into ticking to make mattresses. Jones noted that another layer in the mattress might be duck down. In those days, no one gave a thought, she added, to the possibility that a person might be allergic to the straw or to the duck feathers.

＊＊

---

[22] Ibid.

Sister continues after her mention of the number fed on threshing day, only to say that the company ate well; she does not give the menu, beyond the mention of iced tea. (It's unclear whether she feasted on ice cream, too, as well as the tea—probably so, for regular cream was likely to be regularly available.) She does want Martin not to protest that his coming for a visit will add to the work. "The work has to go on," she says, whether he was visiting or not. Surely, he can see the logic in that argument, though she has just written, in an earlier sentence, that his coming will mean a "rest" from usual labors.

> *These folks feed a person here. I am growing fat on ice tea and other good things. You know we don't have much ice at home it is so far to go for it. I'll just tell you now you better take on enough ice tea, cream and such to satisfy you before coming to the Mts.* <u>*We*</u> *feed on* <u>*Water*</u>*. But I should not try to tell you what all we are going to have for I'm afraid you will be shocked soon enough. And of course we are going to have a jolly good time[;] while you are there will be a rest for us. I think you are the most thoughtful boy I have ever been in company with, you must not go to studying about being trouble for us. It will all be the pleasure for the work has to go on if you were not here just the same[,] you know.*

> *Think I will want you to arrive at Maysville and home about the 30th of July and I don't know as I'm going to let you go back there at all, so you must not buy a return ticket.*

> *Called home yesterday. Irene said there was a letter there . . .* [indecipherable, from a page fold, not from the handwriting] *from Stockbridge so I can hardly wait to get home to read it.*
> *Take care of yourself [and] be good.*

> *Love from*
Sister

The next letter is undated; it was written in the fall; I'm assigning it the year 1915, the same year as the letter from Ashland, because it was written from home, where, as far as we can tell from the letter's content, she was still living. (A year later she will be boarding with a family in Lula and teaching at a school there.) This letter begins with a plea that Martin overlook the fact that again she must write in pencil. "Don't look at it closely," she writes. Oh, dear—he will have to, won't he—if he wants to read it.

Mon. morning

Dear Martin,

I thought once I would not write until I could get some more paper and a bottle of ink but you know we do not go to town very often and so I don't know when I will have a chance to get any and so I am using this instead of waiting, but please don't look at it very closely. You will have to look closely in order to read this, won't you?

Well, the convention is over and the result of it is pleasant memories. Both days the singing was excellent, some of the best we have heard and everyone seemed to be enjoying it. There were so many folks there yesterday one could hardly turn around. A lot more than when you were here. I saw a number of old friends and most of the folks there that you know. But of course there were some absent. I guess you would have enjoyed it, I did, but when we got home last evening I was awfully tired. All day occasions always tire me but I was unusually tired last night and I don't feel rested from it yet. Neal was asking about you.

Did you notice the sunset last night? It was the most beautiful one I ever viewed. I sat and watched it till the darkness drove it away and I wondered if you were seeing the beauty of it too. I love the scenes of sunset and they are more beautiful in the fall than any other season of the year. Mother

> *got up Sat morning telling her dream. Said she dreamed of being at . . .*

There this page ends, and we have no other. What do we, who can't even be sure of the letter's date, know from this truncated message? It seems that Sister has known Martin for some time; he is one of any number of friends she usually sees at conventions. When he misses one, people ask her about him—a fact that makes it clear that they often attend together, that there is a special closeness between them, even if we have no name for that closeness. We wonder, of course, who the Neal is, and we note that Sister is comfortable writing to Martin about her mother; we can assume that her mother and her friend are well-disposed the one to the other.

This undated letter is the second in the collection in which someone writes to Martin about a convention—Mack Carnes had gone to one, traveling from Wilmore, Kentucky, to Meridian, Texas. Every Protestant denomination seems to have had conventions—local, state, national. There were state and national Sunday School Conventions, as well, and those seem to have crossed denominational lines. Sister appears to be writing about a local convention, held near enough to her home for her to reach on a Saturday morning and return for a second day.

Since Sister mentions only the singing, let's take her at her word, incomplete though we may find the word, and assume that she is talking about a singing convention. At the end of the nineteenth and the beginning of the twentieth century, singing conventions were very popular in rural America, particularly in the rural South.

There were singing conventions in churches near Sister's home. Some decades earlier, the "Singing Convention in Walnut Church, July 30, 1888" made headline news in the *Jackson Herald* (Jefferson, Georgia). "The Jackson County Musical Convention met . . . today [the article reads] and was called to order by the president."[23] After an opening song and prayer, the convention proceeded to organize—organizing included naming a committee on credentials and receiving both written and oral reports from church groups, usually the Sunday schools of those churches that comprised the convention's membership. There were also singing choirs, and news stories carried names of the organists and pianists who accompanied the choirs. Membership in singing choirs and singing conventions must surely have overlapped.

There was a singing convention in one little Georgia town with thousands of attendees; hundreds were there for dinner-on-the-ground, and the politicians came too, of course. Trains ran routes to facilitate people's getting to the convention, with one town—the point of origin for the train trip—practically deserted as everybody went off to the singing. This convention had begun in 1875 as the South Georgia Singing Convention, led by William Jackson Royal, a music teacher at the Irwin Institute (Irwin County—Ocilla the county seat). As the convention grew larger, people became convention members with class structure, badges, and dues (five cents). Members came from all denominations and from all the churches in the area, and the various churches took turns as host church for the event. Within a few years, the members voted for a name change and in 1893 the convention became the Royal Singing Convention.

The members also voted to purchase several city blocks near the Baptist Church in Mystic, a small town in Irwin County, and the convention erected a tent on the property in 1912. The tent could accommodate the thousands; after it was destroyed by tornado in 1916, the convention met in a warehouse, then in 1919 it built a tabernacle. The Royal Singing Convention, which met each July, probably publicized the fact that songbook publishers would be on site during at least some days of the convention. By 1930, publishers were selling two hundred thousand books each year at the various singing convention sites. The songbooks were the

---

[23] "Singing Convention In Walnut Church[,] July 30[,] 1888." *Jackson Herald.* August 2, 1888. In Jackson County Historical Society News, Vol. 7, No. 1 (October 1999), 4.

shape-note songbooks; printed in either the four-shape (fa-sol-la-mi: ascending scale, fa, sol, la, fa, sol, la, mi, fa) or the seven-note pattern. The seven-note pattern, with shapes the same for the four notes, fa, sol, la, and mi, is the do-re-mi system, familiar to those of us who listened as Julie Andrews and the movie's von Trapp children joyfully sang it in *The Sound of Music.*

To prepare oneself for full enjoyment of the singing convention experience, one would want a songbook. It would be helpful also to have attended a singing school beforehand; the founders of the earliest conventions were likely to be singing schoolmasters, as "Uncle Billy" Royal had been. The schools varied in length, from an afternoon to a day to a weekend. For those who had the time, or for those who were especially talented or especially interested, the singing schools would last a week or more, with a two-week course the most common.

The Royal Singing Convention met for eighty-five years, ending only in 1977; today in the town of Mystic nothing remains of the tabernacle; there is in its place a nice outdoor memorial—platforms and statuary. There is a Library of Congress online site with photos of the tabernacle—no enclosing walls; long pews; sturdily built supports, the supports nicely painted (white). A similar structure could be found at any number of camp meeting sites throughout the state and region.

The singing conventions were seedbeds for Southern Gospel Music, and some of the earliest commercial successes in the recording industry come out of the genre. One of the earliest such stories comes from Braselton, Georgia, in Sister's Jackson County. The group making the recordings was Smith's Sacred Singers, led by J. Frank Smith, who is identified as a Methodist "teacher." That identification is a little suspect, for teachers were not normally identified by sectarian labels. Whoever supplied the term might have meant "preacher," though that label would also have been inaccurate. Another member of the group was a preacher, but I cannot find evidence to support the Methodist affiliation.

Whether J. Frank Smith taught full time or not, he did conduct a singing school. A photograph shows the singing school to have been held at a schoolhouse, and the usual accompanist for the singing group—and probably for the singing school as well—was the wife of the Braselton school's principal. Perhaps Smith and she were professional colleagues. Smith Sacred Singers were recorded in Atlanta in 1926 by a national label. The two sides of the first record were "Picture from Life's Other Side" and "Where We'll Never Grow Old"; the record sold well and "touch[ed] off an interest in recording rural gospel music on the part of the major record labels." [24] Smith's Sacred Singers recorded at least one hundred sides. The conjecture is that that record sales were good because the group was well known through its participation at the various singing conventions in Georgia and surrounding states.

Where a scholarly report on the singing conventions meets the story of Martin and Sister's friendship is in the following account. The author is writing about the Royal Singing Convention for *The Georgia Historical Quarterly*, in a 1972 issue:

> In isolated rural Georgia, the Convention provided a place for budding romance. Of course, young people went with their various classes to sing, but 'people have to court, you know.' The local paper often contained remarks concerning events at Sings which led to new matches. One of the correspondents of the Ocilla *Dispatch* inquired in his column "Which young man was the worst disappointed last Sunday when two other fellows took their best girls home from the sing?" Another writer [noted that] "Every fellow and his girl . . . are going to attend the singing at New Hope next Sunday."[25]

---

[24] "Smith Sacred Singers." Discogs.com.https://www.discogs.com/artist/2649935-Smiths-Sacred-Singers. Smith Sacred Singers' recordings may be found on You Tube; one presentation also includes photographs and newspaper articles.

[25] Karen Luke Johnson, "The Royal Singing Convention, 1893-1931: Shape Note Singing Tradition in Irwin County, Georgia." *The Georgia Historical Quarterly*, no. 4 (1972), 504.

* * *

Was their friendship—Martin and Sister's—a budding romance? The last letter we have from Sister leaves no reason to think that it was, beyond our being so charmed by the young woman that we wish it to have been. The letter carries no date. It was found in an envelope with a postmark that raises questions, more than it provides answers. The post office name cannot be read (the letter would have been posted from Lula, probably). The date is a November date—23, 28, 29, bottom half of the last digit unclear; there is no year visible.

Sister has newly arrived at the home of a family with whom she will board while teaching school; she is trying to get the school organized. A November date may not be late for that, since the opening of school awaited the end of the harvest season, and a November start date was relatively common for the beginning of a term. But if the year is 1916 (which I think probable)—and even if it isn't—a late November date with no mention of Thanksgiving (Thanksgiving in 1916 was on November 25) or plans for Christmas observances is just not what one would expect from Sister. She does, however, note that there is a fire in the parlor of an evening, and she mentions playing tennis during the winter, which apparently is soon to be upon them.

Sister is boarding with Reuben and Mary Boling, an elderly couple, he a Civil War veteran. They live in the Golden Hill community outside the town of Lula. Lula, like Sister's Maysville, straddles a county line, the counties being Hall (county seat, Gainesville) and Banks (county seat, Homer). Golden Hill is in Banks County; therefore, I am going to assume that Sister's school was in Banks County, and that it was probably in Golden Hill. There is a list of twenty-eight schools in Banks County in 1909, but not a one carries the Golden Hill name. There was a McKinney Boling teaching in nearby Hollingsworth in 1860, and there was still a Hollingsworth School in 1909 and a Liberty Hill School located also in Hollingsworth. If the school was in Hollingsworth and if the Boling who taught there was Reuben Boling's brother, those seem to be things Sister would have mentioned. The two Boling men, Reuben, seventeen years old in 1860, and McKinney, the schoolteacher, thirty years old that year—and already married—lived in adjacent households. The two will be enlistees in Company H, 34th Regiment, Georgia Volunteer Infantry, Army of Tennessee, when the war comes.[26] The brotherly relationship seems likely. But Sister can't tell us everything in one letter, and maybe the family wasn't yet sharing Civil War stories or family history with the newly arrived teacher.

Going back in time—earlier than Sister's arrival in Golden Hill—we find in an 1890 Georgia Department of Education annual report that all that was required for a schoolhouse in Banks County was that it be "good enough to winter a cow."[27] When Sister describes her schoolhouse, the only thing she remarks upon is the plants in the schoolyard; we will assume that the building set in that yard was sturdier than any building of an earlier decade might have been. It is to be noted that she does name a school building; the naming indicates that the school is not meeting, as many were, in a church.

Sister is not going to be crass enough to write about salary, but teachers in Georgia's "common schools" were almost everywhere poorly paid. In Clayton County, for instance, a Black teacher at the time would have earned ten dollars a month—less than the wage of a field hand. Payment to teachers might be made quarterly rather than monthly, and then payment might come months later than it was due. Teachers would sometimes take out loans against their promised salaries, turning over vouchers to lenders. One year the state set a cap on the rate at which it would discount the paper submitted for redemption by the loan sharks. "Laborers who cleaned the streets in Atlanta not only received higher wages

---

[26] Jessie Julia Mize, *The History of Banks County, Georgia, 1858-1976*. (Homer, GA: Banks County Chamber of Commerce, 1977), Schools, 115-116; Confederate army regiments, 145 and 149.

[27] James C. Bonner, "The Development of Public Education, 1868-1904." *A History of Public Education in Georgia: 1734-1976*. Oscar H. Joiner, gen ed. (Columbia, SC: The R. L. Bryant Co., 1979), 107.

[than teachers]," the State Commissioner for Education reported in 1901, "they received them at the end of each week."[28] The street cleaner was also paid for three hundred days of work; the teacher might have been paid for as few as one hundred.

The common school was the elementary school. Laws laid out specifics about their location in the rural areas, with the goal of making the common school as widely accessible as possible. In the early records, we find them named "ambulatory schools," located close enough for farm families' children to walk to. High schools were found only in towns and cities; many were private schools; if public, they were likely to be funded by subscriptions that supplemented the municipal tax assessment. Always underfunded, the common schools depended on specified sources for money: Western and Atlantic Railroad profits and rentals (the railroad was state-owned); poll tax; convict hire receipts (until the convict hire system was abolished); inspection fees (fertilizer and oil); taxes on liquor; and taxes on shows and entertainments (fairs and circuses). These monies the state distributed; some counties, labeled "pauper counties," received more revenue than they raised.

The common schools had a common curriculum, and teachers were licensed to teach based on their ability to pass examinations in the subjects they would be expected to teach—orthography, reading, writing, arithmetic, English grammar, geography. A candidate scoring less than 50 percent in any area was supposed to be denied a license, but, where there was need for a warm body willing to sit behind the desk, the examination system was sometimes found to be rather lax. A beginning teacher too often had had no more schooling than that offered by the common school. The county school commissioner in the earliest years, before standardization, would make out the examinations, grade them, and conduct the interviews. A score of seventy on the examination earned one a one-year license (a third-grade license); eighty, a two-year license (second grade); ninety, a three-year license (first grade). How many teachers do you suppose went around talking

---

[28] Ibid, 121-122.

about their third-class licenses? The first-class license, even if one scored at the ninetieth percentile upon first examination, had to await one year's experience in the schoolroom.

Aspiring teachers—these probably aiming for an assignment to a high school (originally called middle schools, in the "middle" between elementary and college)—could be tested in other subjects as well. Among the subjects on which candidates for the license could be tested beyond the common school curriculum were these: United States history, algebra, geometry, physiology, natural philosophy, chemistry, bookkeeping, music, drawing, gymnastics, elocution, school law of Georgia, and the theory and practice of teaching. But one wonders how many exams in specialized areas were ever administered.

For the common school, ordinary folk might not have wanted their teachers to have too much learning. Lula M. Hughes, for example, who started teaching in Bullock County (Statesboro) in 1906, reported that she needed some help from her uncle in recruiting students for her first assignment. There were ten pupils already enrolled, but the minimum number required was fifteen. Her uncle knew a family with five children; as luck would have it, the family lived near the school. "Well," the father of the five said, when he was approached about enrolling them, "I hear that woman teaches the world is round, and I don't want my children learning no such nonsense. We all know the world is flat." Her uncle (Holcomb was his name) replied, "Oh, Lula's highly educated. She's been to college and she can teach it both ways."[29]

The story is just too delightful to receive as anything other than apocryphal, and Hughes is not reporting it—decades later, with a sort of wink to her story-telling uncle—as if the remark had been made to her. Even apocryphal stories, however, might contain an observation worth pondering. Teachers who worried that parents had scant interest in advancing learning might have had reason for the worry. The first compulsory attendance law came a decade

---

[29] Ruth Wynn Aultman, ed. *Reflections of Georgia Retired Teachers*. (Macon, Georgia: Georgia Retired Teachers Association, 1976), 15.

later than Lula Hughes's first year of teaching, just as Sister was entering into her first year in Banks County, yet we find Sister having to make a recruiting effort. She adds this comment after a visit in one home: "I'm afraid that he [the father] is none too much interested in their well being." The statement is not a thoroughgoing assessment of his parental care; all she has been writing about is school enrollment, and she had not found him to be much interested in making schooling available to his children.

Sister also notes for some families a "distressing poverty." The attendance law of 1916 required children between the ages of eight and fourteen to attend school for four months. In the last years of the nineteenth century, 16 percent of the state's population was enrolled in the common schools. That figure was somewhat reasonable, since it approached the 20 percent population share the age group represented in the total population, though the 4 percent gap meant thousands left illiterate. And the 0.5 percent of the population in high school was not at all comparable to that age group's representation in the total population, which was about 8 percent.[30] There were two reasons for the low high school enrollment: If they lived outside the towns, young people would have had no high school easily accessible to them, and their labor was likely to have been needed on the farm or about the house.

Even for younger children, those of the age to be served by the common schools, families might have to make some sacrifices to get them into school. Some families might have been too poor, for example, to provide their children with any of the incidental costs of school attendance, such as the purchase of textbooks. Most counties tried to operate schools only on state-supplied funds; others supplemented those funds with local taxes and patrons' contributions. A law in the 1930s said that the state would pay for

---

[30] Bonner, "Development of Public Education," *History of Public Education in Georgia*, 137, and Thomas D. Snyder, ed.. *120 Years of American Education: A Statistical Portrait*. Table 1: "Population by age and race, live births, and birth rate, 1790-1998," National Center for Educational Statistics, 1993, p. 11. https://nces.ed.gov/pubs93/93442.pdf.

textbooks, but there must have been scant funding for that because it was only in the 1940s that issuing free textbooks became standard practice.

The minimum length of a school term was three months; the nine-month school year became the norm only in the second decade of the twentieth century, maybe later in some districts. In the nineteenth, there might have been a five-month term; that was the case in one county where the school board anticipated two terms in the calendar year, encouraging student learning—and allowing the teacher a better income from two terms of work, rather than one. A summer term might find a college student sitting behind the desk, using the school system for his or her own long-term goals—which did not include staying permanently in the schoolhouse.

Ministers sometimes served as schoolmasters; if schools were in session during an August revival with its daytime services, students would accompany their teacher to the service. (Maybe the service came to them if the sanctuary was serving as their schoolroom.) There were also times when country doctors kept school. The doctors would have welcomed the pay, even if it was a long time coming, since they might have been receiving only small remuneration from their medical practices. Far too many farm families could pay only with farm produce, a sort of barter for services rendered.

There were efforts throughout the period to improve the quality of education by providing avenues through which teachers could improve their competencies. There were County Normal Institutes, which met in the county seats; some predated the 1892 law that made them mandatory. Teachers were expected to attend one week in the summer and one Saturday each month—all sessions paid for from their own pockets. Those who did not attend were penalized; the penalty was payment of a fine; the fine was to be used to provide books for their professional libraries. (I found no account of how many books were thus purchased.) The Saturday sessions were soon enough dropped. The Peabody

Education Fund was used to help defray expenses for some ten-day regional institutes in the early 1890s—for hiring directors and instructors, not for paying stipends to the teachers attending the sessions. In those years, the state was also opening Normal Schools—the earliest the Georgia Normal and Industrial College, GN&IC, a college for women, in Milledgeville (1889) and the Georgia Normal School, this one coeducational, in Athens (1890). The normal college offered a four-year program, the first two years, a high school curriculum; the last two, general and professional education courses. An 1898 law provided for granting a first-grade license based on college credits alone, without the examination, though the examination requirement was soon reinstated.

In 1914, State School Supervisor, M. L. Duggan, after surveying the schools in Rabun County (to the northeast of Banks, Clayton the county seat) outlined what Georgians should expect from their public schools:[31]

I. The Teacher.

1. Good Teaching. 2. Good Order and Management. 3. First Grade Certificate. 4. Full, Neat, and Accurate School Register [the attendance record]. 5. Daily Program Posted in Room. 6. Teacher's Manual on Desk.

II. Grounds.

1. Good Condition. 2. Playgrounds. 3. School Garden. 4. Separate Sanitary Closets.

III. Building.

1. Painted Outside. 2. Plaster, or Ceiled and Painted. 3. No

---

[31] T. E. Smith. "Building on the Framework, 1905-1937." *A History of Public Education in Georgia*, 228-229.

Leaks. 4. Windows Without Broken Frames. 5. Cloak Rooms. 6. Good Doors with Locks and Keys. 7. Clean and well-kept.

IV. Equipment.

1. Patent Modern Desks. 2. At least 20 lineal feet of Blackboard per Room. 3. Building Comfortably Heated and Ventilated. 4. Framed Pictures on the Wall. 5. Dictionary, Maps, and Library. 6. Sanitary Water Supply

V. Associated Activities.

1. Manual Arts, Corn, Canning, Poultry, or Cooking Clubs

VI. Salary of Teacher.

1. At least $40 per month.

VII. Term

1. At least seven months.

It is to be supposed that the requirements outlined by Mr. Duggan, minimal though they seem, might not everywhere have been in evidence. Where standards were being met, as in Rabun and in Wayne County in southeast Georgia (county seat, Jesup), the counties were supplementing state revenues with local taxes. Beyond local taxes, though, there were also appeals to patrons of the schools. We will note Sister as she begins a new school term bemoaning the poverty of some families even as she accepts the promise from some (and it seems they might be the same families) to send in their fees. Sister has a kind and tender heart, however, in her concern for children in the Lula area. Her concern reminds one of the stories of Martha Berry and other education heroes of the period.³² She tells Martin, for instance, that there were some who were a little too old for her school, whom she is going to teach free of any charge. Sister's letter begins, though, with depictions of her new setting—the home of the family with whom she is boarding and some quick depictions of the family's members.

Lula, Ga. R. 3
Sat. Night

Dearest Martin,

[A long indent] *When I came up here to hunt a boarding place I had such a time finding one that I had almost lost hope of finding one and had made up my mind to give it up if I failed to get in here, but a little to my surprise they accepted me and I was tired I did not think to make inquiry about the mail route so that is why I was unable to tell you in my last letter.* [Whew, for the run on sentence.] *And I kept regretting it because I thought you* (sic) *not knowing my address [that you] would not attempt to write this week and I felt very lonely Wednesday without your letters.* [It must have been a usual occurrence to have a letter from him on the Wednesday.] *But imagine my joy when I came in Friday afternoon and Mrs. Boling says "Here's lots of mail for you," and my eager eyes fell on your handwriting* [there is no period] *first I smiled appreciation in answer to her and hurried off to my room to devour its contents. I really would be very[,] very lonely without your letters. A number of times this week I've been tempted to write you but I was afraid to be sending you so many letters without hearing from you for I wanted them to prove otherwise than disgusting to you. But you have such a frank way of doing things yourself that it makes me ashamed*

---

³² Two maiden aunts of Margaret Mitchell's, daughters of her maternal grandparents, the Philip Fitzgeralds, conducted a school on the Fitzgerald farm in rural Clayton County. "All the pay they received was the satisfaction of helping, which to them was pay enough." (J. Ellis Mundy, *Around a Town Named for Jones.* Jonesboro, GA., 1973), 78. A similar story might have been found in many locations throughout the state.

of my own actions sometimes. Now I wonder if you will just let me write you any old time and not care, for it is company for me? I get so dreadfully lonesome sometimes! So if I chance to write oftener than my mother thinks is good form, you just say, oh well, she's doing it for pleasure.

Sister makes no breaks for paragraphs; though I didn't make one for her above, I think I will now:

Mr. and Mrs. Boling are very pleasant old people. They have raised eleven children and they are all married except two boys. One single son [is]a dentist at Cornelia who Mrs. Boling says is 34 years old and Ernest [who] is 24. Mr. Boling served in the war [the Civil War, which had ended 50 years earlier]. *These people are not very talkative except sometimes Mrs. Boling talks more freely than the men. Ernest never says anything to me* [there is a caret to place "to me" above the line] *unless I ask him a question. Sun. when Father and Mother were here Mr. Boling asked them if I talked much and they said not much and so Mr. Boling and all had a hearty laugh over it for [they] said they don't either and I've found it true[,especially] of Ernest. He seems so timid and shy that it makes me feel uncomfortable and sorry for him. The Lord knows I'll not bite him. He likes to read and I had a number of books along so I provided him with reading matter. It has grown to be a custom of evenings when I return to find a fire in the parlor and I read awhile before supper and he comes in from work* [his work is never identified] *and takes up his books too, so when Mrs. Boling calls to supper she sees me on one side the center table and he on the other with our eyes fixed on our Books* (sic). *We return from the supper table and resume our same position and remain so untill* (sic) *we retire scarcely speaking thru out* (sic) *the evening. Mr. and Mrs. B remain in the dining room. Sometimes on my way to and from school I get to studying about how rediculous* (sic) *we (Ernest and I)* [caret and insert,

> again] *act toward each other that I have a hearty laugh all to myself. You see[,] I'm not pressing him for conversation more than thru politeness and the truth is I don't notice it so much at the present time for I'm so interested in my reading. I do not find him an unpleasant companion but I like to be enough alike in common to be agreeable and yet different enough to be interesting. I guess it would be lonesome and awkward for us if it were not for the books. I've read three big books and two magazines inside of the last week. Ernest has gone to his lodge tonight* [lodge not identified] *so Mr.. and Mrs. Boling are sitting in here. I think you would like Mr. Boling.*

Maybe there's a paragraph break here, even if there's no indentation to mark it. After mentioning the beauty of the place—I assume it is the Boling's home, or its siting, that she means—Sister moves on to writing about her school and her pupils.

> *The view from here is very beautiful. I hope you can see this place next year. School has been small this week and so I have had a very good rest for I can scarcely call this week work with so few, yet they have gotten a nice start[,] those who did come. Next week I will have quite a number. Ernest drove me around to see the patrons this afternoon about seating the schoolroom and we had some fair promises made. I find that there are a number of families who are distressingly poor and my heart goes out in sympathy for those children of such homes. One man told me he did not send his children last year because he couldn't buy books for them. But I'm afraid too that he is none too much interested in their well being, yet for all this he promised to try to get up books and send them and every* [missing word: *fee (?)*] *to help toward the collection. I'm pleased with the outlook of those who have already enrolled and I think I'm going to accomplish much good here. There are some four or five over school age who especially desire to come to school so I have promised to teach them free of charge.*

[I'm making another paragraph break.]

One day I carried the children on a short walk. We went thru the woods and talked about the trees. I found that the children knew them pretty well. We found some of the most beautiful blue gentians I have ever seen so we gathered them for the school room. And I found a big bed of calyx leaves. Have you ever seen any? They are prized highly by the northern people. There is lots of ivy, laurel, and rhododendron near the school house. I am anxious for spring to come to see them in bloom but school may be out when they bloom. You know "John Fox Jr" talks a lot about rhododendrons.

[Now there is a paragraph break, though the new one does not begin with any indentation.]

I'm reading a book now that I like very much and know almost that you would like it. Hope you can read it some time. "David Harwin" by Noyles Wescott. I'll mail it to you (if I knew it wouldn't get lost in the mail) and provided [the word inserted above the line] *you would like to read it.*

Good night.
  [Then added, with no space between the lines]:
This is Sun. morning early and I'm finishing the job I failed to complete last night. A beautiful day this is! What a pity it is wasted when we (you and I) might be spending it so pleasantly. That sounds like a novel don't it (sic)? *Guess I'll read most of the day.*

Remember me kindly to the McMullens when you see them. And give my love to Steve. Where is his cousin from, and why is she so lone-some? With Steve and his mother I think I would not get very lonesome.

How are you liking Miss Bush by this time? I do hope you will have a good time this winter playing tennis.

> *I'm glad Julius likes Miss Howard. I've heard enough of her myself that I really like her too.*
>
> *I think the length of this will make a thorough test of your patience.*
>
> Love from
Sister

I find it interesting, and somewhat surprising, that Sister writes nothing about a church service, even as she is penning a postscript on a Sunday morning. Of course, any country church in Golden Hill, or even a church located in a town so small as Lula, was probably on a circuit and holding worship services only once—maybe twice—a month. Still, I would have assumed church to be a common interest; instead of mentioning church, however, even to explain why she would not be going this Sunday morning, Sister writes about her plan to spend the day reading. Uncle Martin left no evidence that he was a reader; there was no library in his house, for instance, and no books passed on, though he must have owned a Bible. But she has written about writers, as if he would have read them, and about their books, as if they have talked about books—and their authors—often.

I tried to discover something about the writers she mentions upon first reading the letters; at that time, I had no luck. Now I find them—and quite easily. John Fox, Junior, has a museum to celebrate his work and a literary festival named for him too. Many of his novels became well-received movies: *The Trail of the Lonesome Pine, The Little Shepherd of Kingdom Come*—the latest film adaptation of the latter dates to 1961. These titles appeared in *The New York Times* top-ten sellers in 1903, 1904, 1908, and 1909. (Fox's works are available online at Project Gutenberg and at the Internet Archive.) There is also *Blue-grass and Rhododendron: Outdoors in Kentucky*, published in 1901. The title indicates some genre other than fiction; Fox was also a journalist—a war correspondent reporting during the Russo-Japanese War (1905) and, earlier, during the Spanish-American War (1898). In the earlier assignment, he had become friends with Theodore Roosevelt, who, after becoming president, invited Fox to the White House to read some of his stories and play guitar. Fox's novels are set in Kentucky, Virginia, and West Virginia. Some readers probably assumed that Big Stone Gap, the setting for many of his stories, was a fictional place before the museum honoring his work was opened there in 1970. (It's in Virginia.) The Literary Festival, sponsored by the local college and now in its fortieth year, celebrates Appalachian literature. Sister doesn't say that she has read *Blue-grass and Rhododendron*; imagining the rhododendrons in bloom in her new setting simply brings the title to mind.

The *David Harwin* title is just a bit incorrect. Although Sister evidently has a copy with her (she is offering to mail it to Martin, after all), she apparently doesn't think to check its title before mentioning the book. The novel is *David Harum*; it was written by Edward Noyes (not Noyles) Wescott. Wescott, an upstate New York banker with a highly successful thirty-year career in banking, made a banker the hero of his story. At the time of the writing, Wescott was ill with tuberculosis, and he was visiting in Italy, where he had traveled perhaps in search of a cure. Wescott submitted his novel to six publishers before finally finding one to take it. The novel was published posthumously, in 1898. Wescott did have the pleasure of knowing that it would be published; he could probably not have imagined that it would sell one million copies. This book and a shorter one entitled *The Christmas Story* (1900), which seems to have been scripted from a stage play that someone crafted from the novel, are also available online at the Gutenberg Project and the Internet Archive. Motion picture versions of the story were also produced—one starred William H. Crane and another starred Will Rogers.

I wonder what it means that Sister signs the two letters that we have in their entirety with "love from" and that in the last of the three Martin has become "dearest Martin." The letter doesn't read like a love letter; it reads like a letter to a friend. Of course, the friendship may have progressed to a point that needed no protestations of endearment. Such protestations also might have been out of character for the letter writer. As in the other two letters from Sister, what we read is an attempt to share a life and its experiences at a particular point in time and to share it with one whose interests she knows well. Reading this last letter more than a century after its composition leaves the reader with some questions that have no easily found answers. Who are the people whom Sister mentions in her Sunday morning postscript? The McMullens we may think we know. But the other names: Steve — and his cousin and his mother (whom Sister found pleasant) — the Miss Bush, the Miss Howard, and Julius. Who are they?

Then there is the obvious big question — why do we have no other letters from Sister? Why does Sister disappear from Martin's life? For she does seem to have disappeared. The romance novelist would, of course, have Sister and the taciturn Ernest falling in love and Sister breaking her correspondent's heart in ending the relationship with him, the love the protagonist had for her so profound that he lives the remainder of his life as an unmarried man.

Ernest Boling did marry. Ernest's wife, the former Eunice Allen, was eighteen years old in 1920 with a ten-year-old sister named Irene. That sister Irene gave me pause for a moment since it fit with one bit of information we have about Sister. But Eunice would have been too young to be Sister. Eunice did not come from Maysville, either. Hers was a farming family in the Grove River district of Banks County, a community adjacent to the Golden Hill district. It seems rather commonplace to find a marriage partner so close to home, and in a circumstance so similar to one's own. "I like to be enough alike . . . to be agreeable," Sister had noted.

Sister did not identify Ernest's work when she wrote that he had just come in from work to take supper, but, given his father's advanced age, Ernest may well have been managing the family farm. In the 1920 census, after the war, Ernest reported himself to be a farm laborer, probably in his mother's employ, his father having died. There is a "before the war" and an "after the war" story for Ernest, you see, for Ernest, twenty-four years old when Sister meets him, was just the right age for World War I, which had begun in Europe two years earlier. Ernest registered for the draft on June 5, 1917—Congress had declared war against Germany on April 6—and he was drafted into the army. He was in Company E, 167th Infantry Regiment, the 42nd Division. That unit fought in five campaigns in France; Ernest, a private, returned to the States only in April 1919, five months after the war's end, sailing from Brest, France, to Hoboken, New Jersey, with Route 3, Lula named as his destination.

By 1930, Ernest was married—he had married at age thirty-five—and still farming in Golden Hill; he and Eunice were the parents of two little girls. At the time of the 1940 census, there were four daughters; the family was still in Lula, but no longer at the same place it had been living in 1930. Ernest was now a "service laborer," and the employment code makes him a wage or salary government worker, one, moreover, who reports himself to have been unemployed for 156 days during the previous year. The entry lets one know that the Depression years had been hard; it also suggests that at the end of that period he had found employment in one of the New Deal agencies—it was likely to have been on a WPA project. (The WPA was the Works Project Administration; it paid workers principally for the construction of infrastructure—roads, bridges, public buildings.) At the time he died, in 1956, Ernest was living on Myrtle Street in Gainesville. Eunice survived him and continued to live at that address until her own death.

There: I have found more information about Ernest Boling, whom I have no reason ever to have known, than I have found about Martin Wilson, who was my maternal great uncle, in whose community I lived throughout my childhood. Martin did have to register for the draft, I discovered while seeking information on Ernest. The draft law was amended to make the upper age limit forty-five; Martin was already forty years old when he registered in September 1918—almost forty-one. I discover now that I have made him a year younger throughout this account than he was, for he was born in 1877, not in 1878, as most family accounts have it. And the draft card should settle the question we have had in the family about the order of his names: He is A. Martin, not Martin A. And what we have read as "Alonzo" was "Alonza."

Uncle Martin's draft registration card, 1918

The "description of registrant" on the draft card's second page marks him tall and slender. He was tall—this all of us remembered—tall and lanky; rangy: one can imagine a long arc for the extended tennis racket. The picture I carry in my mind is of an unhurried man, almost languid. He would sit for group photos, sometimes in straw hat—more likely the bowler type than the sun-faded, misshaped, sweat-stained farmer's straw. And not often in overalls, either—actually, never in overalls, the attire favored by his younger brother, our grandfather. In every photograph, Martin seems to have on a dress shirt, sometimes a shirt and tie.

More often than hatted, though, he appears bare-headed, and the bare head is bald, or almost so. The face is angular, sharp of feature. I can't remember the eyes; I want to imagine them but cannot. The draft card says that he had lost an eye! Who knew that? The brows are bushy, but that's only because I see him old.

I also see grey, but, at the time of these letters, he must still have had clear blue eyes and hair still light of color, probably a boy's blond that had turned brown and was beginning to grey and to recede. Almost always in the photos (there are disappointedly few of them) his head is tilted. Does vision in only one eye account for that? Or is it usual for so tall a man to list toward the other person, a leaning in the better to communicate, to draw the other person in or to make the other feel one's attentiveness? Because it seems that attentiveness was a gift he gave.

And sometimes withdrew. He withdrew it from the Annas whose friendships with him became broken. I wonder if the kind man, the solicitous one, disappeared into his former judgmentalism after he lost Sister and Mag. There is one official record that might show us a judgmental Martin. When his brother Turner died in December 1940, it was Martin who supplied information for the death certificate. Turner had been living with a woman to whom he claimed to be married, but Martin reported him "widowed." Perhaps Martin disapproved of the relationship; perhaps his response reflected what he thought Turner's children would want recorded; perhaps he deemed it inappropriate to document recognition of what might be termed a "common law" marriage. We cannot know. Maybe in the ordinary interactions of life, however—most of its moments undocumented—in remembrance of friendships past and new ones forming—the kind man remained, the man who might give another the benefit of the doubt, who might offer an encouraging word, supply a helpful boon, or lend a shoulder to lean on.

Family ties and the responsibilities of farm, church, and community must have been enough to make his life a satisfactory one. I wonder, though: Sister did not marry Ernest. Did she die? I searched the Wheeler Family Cemetery on Wheeler Cemetery Road in Maysville for a grave, on the chance that Sister was indeed Katie Wheeler. I found neither a "Katie" nor any variant of that name with her birth year. There was a broken marker "Lun. . ." for Lunie, I assume, whom the census record carries as Lenna, married name Smith. So, the "Irene" I thought I had identified wasn't even an "Irene"—she was "Lunie." Her broken gravestone was an unexpected find in a well-kept ground still receiving family dead. If "Sister" had been a member of this family (a conjecture for which no evidence exists), and if she had died in 1917 or before, still unmarried, this is where the grave would have been laid.

If death did not take Sister out of Martin's life, was there some quarrel between them that could not be worked through? It is certainly possible, of course, that she found someone else—and the story ends as simply as that. Whatever brought the relationship with Sister to an end, I will continue to think that Mag and Sister had known each other, that they had been friends, and that Mag had liked—indeed, Mag had loved—Martin. Did she try to take Sister's place only to find Sister irreplaceable? Or would that, too, have been a scenario only a novelist could write?

To write a memoir of a man barely remembered, replete with speculation, leaves him hardly discovered yet. Except that now we know that, before the age of forty, Martin was a man with varied friendships and that those friendships included young women—any one of whom we could see in the role of aunt to our mother. The man who died before any of us had reached Mattie McMullen's age was approachable to young people, open to their silliness. If we had clearer memories of ourselves in his company, earlier than the years that were soon to take him away, perhaps we would remember shows of fondness, even of amused delight. If family members far distanced from him in time assume a cool aloofness, there is none of that in the younger man. A mercurial temperament in his young adulthood apparently gave way to a steady equanimity. How lovely is the evidence in these letters that there was room in Martin's life for much beyond farm work and family and community life, with such demands and comforts as they might have provided. For him, there was room for reading and singings, for parties and dancing, for taking trips and being welcomed into people's homes, and for the concerns of ultimate moment—life and death and a religion's teachings. There was room for playing tennis. Almost as surprising to us as the tennis playing is the sharing of gossip—and letting down his guard enough so that a correspondent could worry that someone might have hurt his feelings. If friends had a tender regard for him, he must have reciprocated a tenderness; some evidence suggests that the reciprocation had to be learned. Friends—even the mothers of friends—remembered him fondly and wanted to be remembered to him. We glimpse a good conversationalist; we assume an effective writer with correspondents eagerly awaiting his letters and taking pleasure in reading them.

A final query: Was his a happy life? He was a good man, living uprightly—we will hope living fully. What might that life have been if it had had Sister in it?

A family gathering, summer 1941, at Aunt Betty's and Uncle Martin's. Martin standing on the right, leaning onto the steps. Betty, extreme right, second row down. (Their brother, Charlie, is in the center on the row behind Betty.) Mattie, who kept the letters after Betty's death, is on the left behind her husband, W. R. (Buck) Wilson, in overalls. I am the baby on the bottom row, held lightly in check by my mother, Zelma (Jule) Wilson Whitaker.

Martin, third from left, top row, one of the officers of Noah's Ark ME (Methodist Episcopal) Church, Jonesboro, Georgia

Acknowledgments

Joanne Wilson Brown, Mattie Floyd Wilson, and Elizabeth (Betty) Ardella Wilson are three women to whom I owe thanks for making available the letters that are at the heart of this telling of Martin's life. His sister, Betty, to whose memory the book is dedicated, kept the letters among her memorabilia. The family member who was most attentive to Betty's needs in her declining years, who then had possession of the letters, was Mattie. Mattie's daughter, Joanne, has generously shared the letters with other family members and has graciously allowed their use in this book. The book is the second that I've published through BookLogix, a publishing company in Alpharetta, Georgia. I appreciate their editorial and book design expertise; I know that my readers will recognize it, too, for I could not have done this project without them.

Bibliography

Primary Sources

The Atlanta Georgian and Evening News.historicgeorgianewspapers.galileo.usg.edu.

Georgia Department of Health and Vital Statistics. Ancestry.com. Georgia Deaths Index, 1914-1940 (database online). Provo, UT. (Death Certificate for Mills [Miles] Turner Wilson, Dec. 20, 1940.)

Last Will and Testament, Bunard Starr Wilson (1920), in private family collection. Used by permission.

Letters to Martin Wilson (1906-1917), in private family collection. Used by permission.

Noah's Ark church history, in church's informal archive. The archive includes history narratives, membership lists, pastoral appointment lists, photographs, church bulletins, and a copy of one Confederate army communiqué that names the church while it is describing Union troops' movement in the area in 1864. Used by permission.

Photographs, in private family collections. Used by permission.

1915 Tax Digest, Maysville, Jackson County, Georgia. Jackson County, Georgia, Archives, Jefferson, Georgia.

U.S., Army Transport Service, Passenger Lists, 1910-1939. Lehi, UT: USA, Records of the Quartermaster General, 1974-1985. *https://www.ancestry.com>search>collections/611741*.

U.S., Census Reports at
https://www.ancestry.com>search>categories/35/
- Banks County, Georgia, 1910, 1920, 1930.
- Clayton County, Militia District 1088, part (the part being the area outside the city of Jonesboro, Georgia), 1900, 1910, 1920.
- Habersham County, Georgia, 1910, 1920.
- Hall County, Georgia, 1940.
- Henry County, Georgia, District 42, 1870; Militia District 486, 1910, 1920.
- Jackson County, Georgia, 1900, 1910.

U. S., World War I Draft Registration Cards, 1917-1918. https:*www.ancestry.com>search>collections/6482*.

U.S., Headstones. Application for Military Veterans, 1925-1968. *https://www.ancestry.com>search>collections/2375*

Secondary Accounts

Annual Report of the American Missionary Association (Congregational Church). The Association 1917. Report of the Bureau of Women's Work. "Educational Work. The South," books.google.com.

Aultman, Ruth Wynn, editor. *Reflections of Georgia Retired Teachers.* Macon, Georgia: Georgia Retired Teachers Association, 1976.

"The Atlanta Georgian and Evening News." *http://en.wikipedia.org/wiki/The_Atlanta_Georgian.*

Baker, Ray Stannard. "A Race Riot, and After." *The American Magazine*, LXVIII, No. 6, April 1907. Available online at digitalbabel.hathitrust.org

Bonner, James C. "The Development of Public Education, 1868-1904." *History of Public Education in Georgia, 1734-1976*. Joiner, Oscar H., general editor. Columbia, SC: The R. L. Ryan Press, 1979, 69-147.

Chambers, Richard J. "The Early History of Maysville." Unpublished paper. Read at Jackson County Historical Society, July 1986. Available at Jackson County Archives.

"The Conversion of 'Uncle Bud' Robinson." At *https://jawbonedigital.com>conversion-uncle-bud-robinson/*. April 6, 2017. Chapter Two of Morrison's autobiography, *My Life's Story*.

Daniel, David H. "Gospel Singing Conventions." *New Georgia Encyclopedia*. November 15, 2013.

Davis, Aaron. "*John Fox Jr. (1862-1919),*" Encyclopedia Virginia, Virginia Humanities. (2014, May 24).

"Demorest, Georgia." *https://en.wikipedia.org/wiki/Demorest,_Georgia*.

Dewan, Sheila, "100 Years Later, a Painful Episode is Observed at Last," The *New York Times*, Sept. 24, 2006 at http://www.nytimes.com

"Edward Noyes Wescott." *www.britannica.com/biography/Edward-Noyes-Wescott*.

"Edward Noyes Wescott." https://en.wikipedia.org/wiki/Edward_Noyes_Wescott

"Flippen, Georgia."
https://en.wikipedia.org/wiki/Flippen,_Georgia

"Folwstown, Georgia."
https://en.wikipedia.org/wiki/Fowlstown,_Georgia.

"The 40th Annual John Fox Jr. Literary Festival," Mountain Empire Community College, Big Stone Gap, Va., mecca.edu.

Gary, Angela and Jana Adams. *Our Time and Place. A History of Jackson County, Georgia*, Mike Buffington, editor. Jefferson, Georgia: Main Street Newspapers, Inc., 2000

Gillespie, N. Evie. "History of Demorest Methodist Church." Unpublished paper [1951]. https://s3-us-west-2.amazonaws.com/pittarchives/mss028/pdf/Demorest.pdf.

The Heritage of Habersham County, Georgia. 1807-2000. Habersham County Heritage Book Committee, 2001.

The History of the City of Riverdale. N.p. [Jonesboro, Georgia], n.d. [1963]. Available only at Clayton County Library, Battlecreek Road, Jonesboro, Georgia, in its Reference Section.

"Holiness Movement.
https://en.wikipedia.org/wiki/Holiness_movement.

"Homer, Georgia."
https://en.wikipedia.org/wiki/Homer,Georgia/wiki/Homer_Georgia.

Hughes, John Wesley. "The Origins of Asbury College." https://www.asbury.edu/academic/resources/library/archives/biographies

Hunnicutt, George Frederick, editor. *Southern Crops. As Grown* and Described by Successful Farmers and Published from Time to Time in the Southern Cultivator. [Atlanta, GA: The Cultivator Publishing Company], 1908. Available at books.google.com.

Jackson County Historical Society News. Vol. 7, No. 1, October 1999. Reprints of two articles on singing conventions and singing choirs: "Singing Convention in Walnut Church[,] July 30[,] 1888," *Jackson Herald*, August 2, 1888, and "Jackson County Singing Choir Met at Walnut Fork Church on December 9," *Jackson Herald*, December 10, 1906.

Jackson County Historical Society News. Vol. 15, No. 4, July 2008, "Railroads." *Jackson County Historical Society News* is now available at sites.rootsweb/com/~gajackso/indexto . . . (The index is by volume, number, and date, but it does not indicate principal topic for any given issue.)

Jackson, Karen Luke. "The Royal Singing Convention, 1893-1931: Shape Note Singing Tradition in Irwin County, Georgia," *The Georgia Historical Quarterly*. no. 4 (1972): 495-509. www.jstor.org/stable/40579460.

Jones, Ethelene Dyer. "On the Farm. Threshing Times," Excerpt from *Through These Mists. Early Settlers of Union County, Ga. Their Descendants, Their Stories, Their Achievements. Lifting the Mists of History on Their Way of Life* (2007), reprinted in the Union Sentinel, Blairsville, Ga., July 28, 2011 at rootsweb.com > ~ gaunion.

Kinnell, Matt. "E. Stanley Jones." https://www.asbury.edu/academics/resources/library/archives/biographies.

Kinnell, Matt. "Henry Clay Morrison." https://www.asbury.edu/academics/resources/library/archives/biographies.

Kinnell, Matt. "John Wesley Hughes." https://www.asbury.edu/academics/resources/library/archives/biographies.

Kuhn, Cliff and Merritt, Carole. "The Race Riot of 1906." From "Georgia Stories." Georgia Public Broadcasting. Originally broadcast 03/12/1994, rebroadcast, 12/13/2019) at gbp.org.

"Lakewood Fairgrounds." https://en.wikikpedia.org/wiki/Lakewood_Fairgrounds

"Lula." cityoflula.com.

"Lula," Wikipedia. https://en.wikipedia.org.

McKinley, Edward H. "A History of Asbury College Chronology." https://www.asbury.edu/resources/library/archives. Archives: A History of Asbury University.

McQuire, Peter S. "Athens and the Northeastern Railroad, Part 1," *The Georgia Historical Quarterly*, Vol. 12, No.1 (March 1934), 1-26, available at http://jstor.org.

Mixon, Gregory and Kuhn, Clifford. "Atlanta Race Riot of 1906." *New Georgia Encyclopedia*.

Mize, Jessie Julia. *The History of Banks County, Georgia, 1858-1976*. [Homer, Georgia]: Banks County Chamber of Commerce, 1977.
Moore, Rob. "Maysville: 'You learn to grow with the people." accessWCUN.
https://accesswdun.com/article/2020/1/863334/maysville-you-learn-to-grow-with-the-people.

Morris, Gene Jr. *True Southerners. A Pictorial History of Henry County, Georgia*. McDonough, GA: The Henry County Record, 2000.

Mundy, J. Ellis. *Around a Town Named for Jones.* [Jonesboro, GA: Historical Jonesboro], 1973.

"1906 Atlanta race riot." https://en.wikipediaorg/wiki/1906_Atlanta_race_riot.

"Our History." [Piedmont University] https://www/piedmont.edu/about_piedmont/history/

Pomerantz, Gary M. *Where Peachtree Meets Sweet Auburn. A Saga of Race and Family.* New York: Simon and Schuster, 1996. The 1906 Race Riot, pp. 72-77.

Reinhardt, Claudia. "Harvesting Wheat," in "Farming in the 1920s" http://livinghistoryfarm.org/farminginthe20s/intro/machine/harvesting-wheat/.

"Riverdale, Georgia." https://en.wikipedia.org/wiki/Riverdale,_Georgia.

"Smith Sacred Singers." Smith Sacred Singers. discogs.com. Several selections from the Smith Sacred Singers are available on YouTube.

Smith, T. E. "Building on the Framework, 1905-1937." *History of Public Education in Georgia, 1734-1976.* Joiner, Oscar H., general editor. Columbia, SC: The R. L. Ryan Press, 1979, 148-280.

Snyder, Thomas D., editor. *120 Years of American Education: A Statistical Portrait.* National Center for Educational Statistics, 1993. https://nces.ed.gov/pubs93/93442.pdf. Table 1. Population by age and race, live births, and birth rate: 1790-1991, 11-13.

Wright, Chip. "Demorest Women's Club." https://npgallery.nps.gov/NRHP/GetAsset/NRHP/08001247_text. Application from Demorest Women's Club to list their clubhouse, the former Methodist Church, on the National Registry of Historical Places.

About the Author

Dorothea Whitaker McAlvin is a retired teacher (history and social studies at the secondary level). In the two decades since retirement, she has devoted time to family (husband, Carl, now deceased, three daughters, eight grandchildren), extended family, church, community, and to research and writing. She has authored another memoir, recently published, that was also based on family letters. A graduate of Young Harris College, with degrees from the Woman's College of Georgia and Georgia State University, she studied one year in France before beginning her teaching career, marrying, starting a family, and undertaking graduate studies. Hobbies and interests include reading, travel, local history, Bible and religious studies, Sudoku and crossword puzzles, and taking classes in all sorts of subjects through lifetime learning institutes. She lives in Hoschton, Georgia, and is now attempting her hand at fiction.

Other Books by
Dorothea Whitaker McAlvin

Sorgum, Jule, and Horsefly. A Memoir. A History.

www.ingramcontent.com/pod-product-compliance
Lightning Source LLC
Chambersburg PA
CBHW071246070526
44583CB00017B/2354